THE CRAFT OF CHRÉTIEN DE TROYES:
AN ESSAY ON NARRATIVE ART

DAVIS MEDIEVAL
TEXTS AND STUDIES

UNIVERSITY OF CALIFORNIA, DAVIS

VOLUME THREE

NORRIS J. LACY

THE CRAFT OF CHRÉTIEN DE TROYES:
AN ESSAY ON NARRATIVE ART

LUGDUNI BATAVORUM E.J. BRILL MCMLXXX

THE CRAFT OF CHRÉTIEN DE TROYES:
AN ESSAY ON NARRATIVE ART

BY

NORRIS J. LACY

LUGDUNI BATAVORUM E. J. BRILL MCMLXXX

ISBN 90 04 06191 6

CONTENTS

PREFACE

In the late Twentieth Century, in the midst of what we could without injustice call a renaissance of medievalism, as new studies of medieval poets and poems appear every day, an examination of the narrative technique of Chrétien de Troyes scarcely requires justification. If Chrétien was not, as some have contended, the creator of the modern novel, he was nevertheless the most important creator of medieval romance and one of the most remarkable writers of the Middle Ages. While his works are not without flaws, he is a superb storyteller, a sensitive poet, a consummate craftsman; and it is that craft—Chrétien's technique and his technical achievement—which will occupy us in this volume.

But perhaps I can best describe the focus of this book by defining first what it is *not*. It is not, for example, a full introduction to Chrétien, his times, and his works. For reasons both practical and theoretical, I have tried to divorce *l'homme* from *l'œuvre*, the historical author from his literary art. It is the latter, the products of literary creation, which are my specific subject, and I shall deal with Chrétien as author only to the extent that he is obviously present as narrator in his poems.

Moreover, I have excluded from this study all philological considerations and questions of manuscript tradition and literary transmission; this exclusion is not intended to imply that such matters are not in themselves important, but only that, with certain obvious exceptions, they are not of consequence for my present emphases. Nor, finally, have I thought it necessary to give a detailed survey of past criticism or to provide a thorough bibliographical tool for readers. I have of course acknowledged all my conscious debts and sources and have offered a number of additional references to related material, but beyond that I have not sought to be exhaustive in my documentation. My focus has remained instead on the texts themselves and on certain critical problems they present. The following chapters, directed to students as much as to specialists, are thus intended as essays in literary criticism, as attempts to describe and analyze certain aspects of Chrétien's narrative technique.

But if I have intentionally excluded much from my study, I have nonetheless taken "narrative technique" in a rather broad sense; the term refers here to the ensemble of methods by which Chrétien assembles his works so as to confer on them the form, meaning, and artistic appeal he is seeking. Consequently, I treat certain subjects—such as thematic concerns and symbolism—that a narrower definition might well exclude but that I consider, for practical reasons, inseparable from Chrétien's narrative methods. Such matters, peripheral but pertinent to technique, are presented in the first chapter, which is explicitly introductory and general, and in the second, itself relatively general. These two brief sections provide the foundation (themes, characterization, and Chrétien's fictional universe) for the more detailed and lengthy discussions to follow. Yet, the early chapters are not merely prefatory, for the precise way the quest functions, the development of characters, etc. are in fact part of the structural elaboration of the work, whereas—conversely—the formal progression is an important element in the elucidation of character or the revelation of meaning. Theme, form, and character constantly refer to one another. For example, the Grail Castle episode leads to Perceval's quest, illuminates his flawed character, excites our interest by the techniques of Chrétien's presentation, and serves as the central structural component of the Perceval sequence. Thus, that episode belongs by rights in all four major chapters. But despite the consequent problem of duplication, the organization of the present study by topic, dividing narrative procedures into their various elements and proceeding from the general to the particular, seems to me to provide the most effective access to the technical aspects of Chrétien's art.

Many of the critical debts I have incurred in the preparation of this volume will be made apparent by my references in the text itself; I am happy to acknowledge others here. First, to my students at the University of Kansas and at UCLA; they provided the first audience for many of these ideas, and in more than a few instances a question or a criticism from one of them led me to define further an approach or a conclusion. It is a pleasure to express my appreciation to them, but unfortunately, naming some of them would constitute an injustice to too many others.

I also owe a debt of gratitude to the National Endowment for the Humanities for a 1975 summer stipend and to the University of Kansas for grants from the General Research Fund in 1975 and 1976; these awards greatly facilitated my research and writing and are most appreciated.

I am grateful to the editors of certain journals, who kindly permitted me to use some material which had previously appeared in print. Chapter II uses sections of "Yvain's Evolution and the Role of the Lion," *Romance Notes*, 12, No. 1 (1970), 198-202, and the following chapter includes "Narrative Point of View and the Problem of Erec's Motivation," *Kentucky Romance Quarterly*, 18, No. 4 (1971), 355-62. Chapter IV uses portions of several earlier studies: "Thematic Analogues in *Erec*," *L'Esprit Créateur*, 9, No. 4 (Winter 1969), 267-74; "Form and Pattern in *Cligés*," *Orbis Litterarum*, 25, No. 4 (1970), 307-13; "Thematic Structure in the *Charrette*," *L'Esprit Créateur*, 12, No. 1 (Spring 1972), 13-18; "Organic

Structure of Yvain's Expiation," *Romanic Review*, 61, No. 2 (April 1970), 79-84.

Finally, my thanks to Professors Sara Sturm-Maddox, who read the entire manuscript, and Glyn Burgess, who read portions of it. I greatly appreciate their kindness and their perceptive critiques.

N. J. L.
July 1976

CHAPTER I

INTRODUCTION: THE CRISIS AND THE QUEST

The quest is one of the most natural and most nearly constant characteristics of the Arthurian romance. It is a fictional vehicle that permits Chrétien de Troyes, or another writer, to regale readers with varied, exotic, and wonderful adventures, to excite their curiosity about the next in the sequence of events, to exercise his own virtuosity as a creator of fiction (not an insignificant consideration for Chrétien), and at the same time to develop and communicate the coherent meaning of his work. As a result, all five of Chrétien's Arthurian romances include quests, and all but *Cligés* exploit them as a major motif and structure. But while the quest may occupy the larger part of a poem, it should not be separated in our minds, any more than it is in the characters', from the reasons for it. All Chrétien's works can be divided, rather crudely perhaps, into "before" and "after." The dividing line between these two parts is the crisis, by which a character realizes his failing and sets out to repair it. Put another way, the character comes to understand what he has been and sets out to become something else. The most succinct example of this is Yvain, who rejects even his own name, because it is associated with what he has been, and wishes to be known henceforth as the Knight with the Lion. He wishes to begin *tabula rasa* and construct for himself a new identity unlike the former one.[1]

A convenient, if oversimplified, statement of the pattern of Chrétien's romances is provided by William Woods.[2] Describing the plot patterns in *Erec et Enide, Yvain, Perceval*, and *Guillaume d'Angleterre*, he notes three significant points in the development of these works. First, the hero achieves a high degree of personal happiness and worldly success in an initial and usually self-contained sequence. Then he is made aware of an error or flaw which invalidates that happiness and success. Finally, in the major portion of the poem, he undertakes a series of adventures in order to correct the error and thereby recover his happiness. Indeed, with only modest changes in his formula, Woods could have included *Lancelot* in his discussion, and even *Cligés* seems to be less a novel situation than a variation on the same one. The hero of the latter romance finds himself at an impasse, rather than in a crisis caused by an error, but the pattern of adventures, the anguish of the characters, and the basic cause of that anguish make *Cligés* resemble the other works in a number of remarkable ways.

Naturally, the crisis can have various causes and take numerous forms, but in practically every case, it is intimately associated with the character's relationship and reaction to the ideals accepted in the Arthurian court. Although most of Chrétien's Arthurian heroes spend relatively little time at Arthur's court, it remains the center of the chivalric universe. The court, with its fame and splendor, dominates the romances and remains constantly present before the hero's eyes, providing inspiration for action and standards for conduct. Acceptance in Arthur's court is a knight's guarantee of fame throughout the world: in *Cligés*, Chrétien speaks of "roi Artus qui lors reignoit/ Et des barons que il tenoit/ An sa conpaignie toz jorz,/ Par qu'estoit dotee sa corz/ Et renomee par le monde."[3] For Alexandre, in the same romance, the crown and wealth of Greece, with Constantinople included for good measure, hold little appeal beside the prospect of being knighted by Arthur (vss. 121-43). The court is the source of much of the good in the world, for it not only provides a vision of sumptuous luxury but it upholds important ideals, from the preservation of social and political order (chivalry is a conservative institution) to the protection by its members of the afflicted and oppressed. Those in need seek out a champion among the best at the court, and their pleas are seldom unheeded, for the court is populated by knights who will leave at a moment's notice and travel to the far reaches of the world to offer aid to a lady in distress. The most eager of such knights is Gauvain; hearing, in *Perceval*, of the lady besieged at Montesclaire, he reacts in typical fashion, leaping to his feet and announcing that ". . . son pooir fera/ De li rescorre, s'i ira" (vss. 4719-20).

The preceding description of the Arthurian court is, I think, accurate as far as it goes, but the eye Chrétien focuses on that court is not entirely uncritical. Honor, glory, and renown naturally accrue to the knight who performs great and admirable exploits. But even at the beginning of Chrétien's work, we can see that a fundamental shift has occurred in the practical application of the courtly ethic: such honor and glory are not only the result but in many cases the purpose of exploits; the knight has ceased to be simply the instrument and has become the end. Erec has already won renown when we first see him, but except for his brief distraction by marital bliss he devotes himself entirely to preserving and increasing his fame. At the beginning of *Cligés*, Alexandre insists:

Maint haut home par lor peresce
Perdent grant los qu'avoir porroient,
Se par la terre cheminoient.
Ne s'acordent pas bien ansanble
Repos et los, si com moi sanble,

Car de nule rien ne s'alose
Riches hom qui toz jorz repose,
Ensi sont contraire et divers.

(vss. 152-59)

In this speech, which will be echoed by Gauvain as he attempts to persuade Yvain to leave his wife, Alexandre argues that the purpose of prowess is the acquisition of fame. The idea of service, which might reasonably be expected to stimulate and justify the knight's exercise of his craft, is nowhere to be found. In answer to Alexandre, his father gives him advice on the surest way to win fame and acceptance at court: win it with largesse. Generosity is the queen of virtues. The story develops as a confirmation of his father's words, for Alexandre stays at court and gives away money until he gains the admiration of all who are there.

Chrétien presents us, throughout his works, a varied picture of chivalry and the court, ranging from theoretical ideals to general precepts to very explicit and precise rules. By the time we come to his last work, knighthood, notably in Perceval's mind but apparently for other characters as well, can be reduced to a kind of chivalric catechism, a series of rules and precepts which can be recited and learned and which, if followed, will bring success and glory. Rules such as "A knight does not talk too much or ask many questions" illustrate just how far chivalry has strayed from its theoretical function and purpose. By now, we are not far removed from Capellanus's rules for love; in both cases, sophisticated ideals have been codified in a list of rules.

It is scarcely surprising that such a code will come into conflict with a knight's moral sense or natural inclination; indeed, in a sense, chivalry is in fundamental conflict with itself, for in its theoretical purpose it is directed away from itself, toward others, while in fact it has become self-centered and self-serving (although without ceasing, in most cases, to serve others accessorily). The means and ends of chivalry have been inverted:[4] feats of prowess, bringing the knight renown and reputation, should have as their legitimate justification the protection and defense of others, but now such defense serves to illustrate the knight's prowess and increase his renown.

This discussion of the crisis might suggest that Chrétien's works constitute an indictment of chivalry, for any time a knight espouses its precepts wholeheartedly, he is inevitably led into error. Writing on *Perceval*, Gallais (p. 43) asserts that "d'un bout à l'autre du roman, Perceval dit non à la cour d'Arthur," and this is part of his evidence that (p. 42) as his works progress Chrétien comes more and more to judge the values accepted in Arthur's court to be inauthentic. I think such a suggestion, though largely valid, requires amplification. It is true that the

Arthurian court represents "culture" in all the senses of that word (Gallais, 42); it is a code to be taught, learned, and followed rigorously by knights. Chivalry, as the court accepts it, is thus an artificial construct. But this cultivated artifact, chivalry, has the power to fascinate, to satisfy, and thereby to become an end in itself, detached from the presumed reason for its cultivation. Arthurian characters repeatedly and erroneously attempt to separate form and content, or form and meaning. The form is the code of knightly conduct: the rules of war and courtesy, the elaborate series of instructions which preceded or accompanied the process of becoming a knight and proving oneself worthy of that title.

It may be correct to suggest that Chrétien judges inauthentic the way the Arthurian code is understood and applied at the court, but we should not go further and assume that he was constructing a persuasive rejection of the Arthurian ethic itself. Not surprisingly, that ethic, in its theoretical conception, is considerably superior to its practical implementation. Chrétien frequently constructs characters or depicts institutions that are less than perfect, but the function of such a practice is normally to emphasize the initial identity of his hero with these characters or institutions and his ultimate superiority over them. In other words, adverse ethical judgments attach implicitly to the Arthurian court, but they do so only in a subsidiary way. In any case, it is clear that Chrétien is not criticizing an ideal as much as he is depicting the perversion of that ideal, and abuses of an institution do not invalidate the institution. Chrétien frequently contrasts the ideal and the actual. He did so at the beginning of *Yvain*, when he announced his intention to recount a story which took place in the "good old days" when love was still what it was supposed to be; now (he says) love is debased and flawed, for it has no true followers (vss. 17-28). In the same way, he contrasts the proper or ideal expression of the chivalric ethic with its real expression, and in so doing he offers, usually in the person of Gauvain, an implied critique of the latter.

Chrétien's last three romances—*Yvain, Lancelot, Perceval*— offer ample evidence of this critique. While the three differ in striking ways, they all provide illustrations of the deleterious effects of a slavish adherence to a learned code of chivalry, when that code and the values attached to it are taken as an end, as their own justification. Yvain, goaded by Gauvain, concludes that the active life and the constant demonstration of valor and prowess are essential pursuits for a knight, but he thereby neglects other legitimate obligations which he has accepted. For him, the form of chivalry, the code, the physical manifestations justify themselves; they provide (as they always do for Gauvain) their own meaning. *Lancelot* is radically different in the relationship the story eventually establishes between love and prowess, but again it is the hero's chivalric pride, his concern for his reputation and for the way a knight *should* react to a particular situation, which determine his response to the dwarf's invitation to ride in the cart and which jeopardize his relationship with Guenevere. With *Perceval* the situation grows in complexity, but also, curiously enough, in clarity. Perceval in his original state is notable for his candor and ingenuousness above all else. His loquacity is comical simply because the climate established with the knights' arrival is dominated by their code, according to which, we shall soon learn along with him, one does not talk too much or ask too many questions. Similarly, subsequent episodes depict a direct confrontation of his nature (instinct or inclination) and his "culture" or adopted code. The opposition is *nature-norreture* (a common motif in the Middle Ages but nowhere developed more precisely or more effectively than here). As we know, it is the code which wins; in his desire to act in a manner befitting a knight, Perceval represses his natural impulse to pose the Grail question, and a catastrophe follows, both for him and for the kingdom he failed to restore. In these cases, the character's negligence of his duty in favor of what he considers "proper" behavior precipitates the crisis and demonstrates ways in which the Arthurian code, like any other, lacks meaning and efficacy in itself. With each poem, Chrétien is engaging in a detailed literary examination of the knight's craft, his duties and obligations, the nature of chivalry itself. Against the background of this highly sophisticated, somewhat rigid code, his characters easily, indeed inevitably, find themselves in situations with which they are unprepared to deal. The conflict they experience may be between love and prowess, as it is most often presented, but such a statement oversimplifies the problem. That conflict is at bottom a confrontation between the basically egotistical cult of physical action and the presumably more passive, unselfish code of love and sentiment, and as I have suggested, it is in some instances (and most clearly in *Perceval*) a conflict between a character's natural (and therefore good) impulse and the action dictated by an artificial and learned code of behavior. These two alternatives (active vs. passive, love vs. adventure) would appear to be mutually exclusive, but in fact, with the exception of *Lancelot*, Chrétien never develops a situation in which the dictates of love are necessarily at variance with those of prowess. Thus the conflict which the characters perceive is generally illusory; it exists only in their own minds. In choosing, for example, love over prowess, Erec makes an erroneous and destructive decision, but the opposite decision would be equally wrong, as Yvain's actions will illustrate. Chrétien's characters are afflicted initially with an "either/or" mentality; they can accept the value of one alternative only by rejecting the other. It is this faulty judgment which precipitates the crisis. The quest, the period of wandering and tribulation which typically follows, then constitutes not only an expiation of the hero's faults but a process of maturing as well, a maturing both of perception and of character. Thus, he "learns his lesson" in two senses: he pays for his error at the same time as he comes to understand it and generally to arrive at a synthesis of what he previously thought to be irreconcilable opposites: the active and the passive life, love and adventure, reason and inclination.

Thus, the hero of romance tends to be both subject and object of the quest. He sets out to achieve a goal, whether it is to find and free the queen, as Lancelot does, or to perform actions which will prove his worthiness of a lady's love, which is Yvain's purpose. But since he cannot achieve that goal unless he *is* in fact worthy, and since he has previously been shown to be unworthy, he himself becomes the real object of his quest. What he is really seeking is himself, his identity, his chivalric vocation; and his ostensible objective, while important, appears at times almost incidental.

Yvain, for example, vows never to relax his efforts and cease his wandering until he regains the love of Laudine, but significantly, he does nothing specific to attract her attention or to impress her with his valor or devotion. But Chrétien's works are peopled with characters who have mysterious access to information; they know things without our knowing how they know. News travels in the Arthurian world, and Yvain can (and must) accomplish his goal *in absentia*. When, as the Knight with the Lion, he has made himself worthy once again of Laudine's love, then Lunete's final stratagem will enable him to resume his marital and amorous joy.

The work in which the subject-object duality of the quest is least emphasized (*Lancelot*) provides another duality which functions in much the same way. The hero has two purposes here, in addition to proving to Guenevere that he can put service and obedience to love above all other concerns. He must find and liberate her, but he is to do the same for the prisoners held in Gorre, a quest which is tied to the former one and which he accomplishes in almost incidental fashion.

The subject-object duality and what I have referred to as the characters' either-or mentality are only two of a large number of oppositions or polarities functioning as axes along which Chrétien organizes his work. This is not to suggest, as it might be taken, that Chrétien sees everything in black and white, that he has a simplistic conception of his characters and their world. It is quite obvious that such is not the case. His heroes are good and upright, but flawed individuals; his villains are evil but often courageous and valorous people. Rather, these polarities provide a play of tensions within the work, tensions which may be related to character, to plot, to motif development, or to structure, but which in any case serve as essential focuses providing much of the dramatic interest of his works. Not only does Chrétien play off one character (usually Gauvain) against another (the hero), but he also exploits the opposition of appearance (illusion) and reality, of *nature* and *norreture*, of concealment and revelation, of haste and delay. These contrasts normally possess both thematic and structural value. Indeed, in the development of the quest situation, one further polarity provides perhaps the major structural tension of the work: that is the contrast between the conventional, predictable, patterned arrangement of events which points toward a definite conclusion and the open, discursive, indefinitely expandable series of episodes which constitute the typical randomness of the quest.

The author remains free to develop the quest with as much variety as he wishes, and in fact much of the appeal of the work will obviously depend on his success in offering his readers an exciting and suspenseful series of adventures. Nonetheless, the idea of a quest implies certain conventions which few authors of romance violate; as summarized by Douglas Kelly, ". . . the knight will usually grant mercy to a defeated opponent, refuse to halt more than one night before achieving his quest, preserve his incognito, and respond to any challenge."[5] As Kelly suggests, it is the hero's response which remains relatively constant; the variety of the narrative occurs in the different forms taken by the threats and adventures he encounters. In fact, it is this tension between sameness and variety, between the gratuitousness of unconnected adventures and the inevitability of the knight's response which gives life and interest, and meaning as well, to the quest. That is, the hero can experience the most bizarre and extraordinary adventures, but his role is to offer a single, constant response to them. This apparent rigidity is a mark of resolve, determination, and devotion, while a response which varied with the situation would be more characteristic of Gauvain, who devotes himself singlemindedly to one task only until another captures his attention.

A brief illustration of the quest form may be offered by *Lancelot*. That hero's quest, in the first part of the work, is unusual in that it precedes (and includes) the crisis. Lancelot seeks Guenevere and errs, in the cart scene, by not doing so with necessary resoluteness. But except for that error, he reacts with immediate decisiveness to the most unusual threats, from flaming beds to sword bridges to other knights. His response in each case is to meet the challenge in the most direct way possible, without the slightest hesitation, and then to hasten on his way to find the queen. It is understandable that he would refuse to hesitate in instances where immediate action will both bring him glory and bring him closer to the queen. Before the cart, however, he hesitates because his own glory requires him to think twice, while his quest should dictate the opposite reaction. This error necessitates an additional quest and an expiation.

The quest is normally unified by the hero's constant response to changing situations, but this thematic uniformity is far from being the only unity of the quest. As we shall see later, the randomness of the hero's adventures (of their subject matter) is balanced by striking correspondences and symmetries among the episodes. But for the moment, the point to be made is that, taken as a group, these adventures bear a relationship not only to each other but to the event or action which brought them about. That is, several of the romances present a system of retribution or expiation whereby the sin not only necessitates punishment, but determines the precise form it is to take.

Readers of Dante will recognize the preceding as a description of his principle of the *contrappasso*. One of the most familiar examples, from the *Inferno*, is the fate of Paolo and Francesca, who, having been caught up in the figurative winds of passion, are doomed to be swept about forever by actual winds, which never allow them rest.[6] Thus, a qualitative correspondence relates the sin and the suffering. Aquinas discussed the *contrappasso*,[7] and Dante used it to perfection, but it is nonetheless a fundamentally simple idea, which we might reasonably expect to find expressed by other medieval poets. What a person sought improperly, he now has in excess; what he did sinfully, he must continue doing forever. In some instances, the *contrappasso* works by contrast; what a character *failed* to do, he must now do in excess. The two elements of this system of retribution are, usually, the qualitative correspondence between crime and punishment and the exaggerated or inverted form the latter normally takes. Three of Chrétien's poems—*Erec*, *Lancelot*, and *Yvain*—offer nearly perfect illustrations of his method.

The principle of the *contrappasso* is applicable only in a general way to the actions of Erec himself. Erec's fault is his *recreantise*; his conjugal bliss with Enide distracts him from his chivalric pursuits, until his reputation begins to suffer. He thus errs by inactivity, and he must then make amends by an excess of activity, wandering in search of adventure and driving himself, despite his wounds, to the limits of his endurance. He even refuses to interrupt his quest at the bidding of King Arthur, objecting:

. . . ."Sire, je n'ai mie
Plaie de coi je tant me duelle
Que ma voie lessier an vuelle."

(vss. 4214-16)

And again:

> Erec respont: "Or est assez.
> Je ai si ceste chose anprise
> Ne remanroie en nule guise."

(vss. 4230-32)

Of course, Erec could have undertaken a long series of adventures to make retribution for any number of offenses, and the opposition of inaction-action could be simply coincidental. However, we should remember that his journey constitutes a test both of himself and of Enide, for she has offended him and must now prove herself. If we turn our attention to her, we see that her offense is that she uttered the words which caused Erec to doubt her love (vss. 2492-2503). Having spoken when she should have remained silent, she is *commanded* now to remain silent, no matter what happens (vss. 2764-2771). Of course, the work carries the speech-silence contrast to still greater lengths, for ironically it is only by disobeying Erec's order that she finally convinces him of her love. The principle underlying the adventures of both characters dictates that the expiation correspond not only in degree but also in kind to the offense.

Chrétien uses the *contrappasso* to still better advantage in the *Chevalier de la charrette*. Lancelot, searching for Guenevere, has an opportunity to find her more quickly by riding in a cart normally used to transport criminals. His offense is not that he rides in the cart, as he concludes, but that he hesitates to do so, reluctant to commit an act contrary to his idea of a knight's honor. The queen mysteriously learns of his hesitation and later punishes him by commanding him to conduct himself foolishly in the tourneys. The *contrappasso* functions here in two ways. First, he must obey her without hesitation, "des qu'ele le comande" (vs. 5856). But more important, having hesitated to commit a shameful act for his love of the queen, he is forced by her to shame himself now in public. In short, shame and dishonor are the retribution for his desire to avoid the shame and dishonor which complete submission to love would have brought him.

A similar parallel relates offense to expiation in *Yvain*. Here the offense is Yvain's failure to return to his wife at the time he had promised; in other words, he allows adventure to distract him from legitimate promises or obligations. His expiation is performed in the service, not of his wife, but of a number of maidens in distress; nevertheless, this expiation conforms in nature to his offense. If the *contrappasso* is operating in *Yvain*, we should then find the hero contracting obligations and subsequently resisting all attempts to distract him from them, and this is precisely the pattern of his later adventures. First, he promises to aid Lunete, who has been condemned to death on his account. He is determined to honor his promise, and when asked to do battle with Harpin de la Montagne, who threatens Gauvain's relatives, Yvain replies:

> "Je m'en metroie volentiers
> En l'aventure et el peril,
> Se li jaianz et vostre fil
> Venoient demain a tele ore
> Que n'i face trop grant demore,
> Que je serai aillors que ci
> Demain a ore de midi,
> Si con je l'ai acreanté."

(vss. 3938-45)

The following day, as Yvain decides that he can wait no longer (vss. 4030-39), Harpin arrives, and Yvain does take time to do battle with him. Yet his decision had been made: he must not fail to return to Lunete, and in fact, he does arrive just in time to save her. Later, on his way back to court to defend a disinherited maiden against her sister's champion, Yvain turns aside briefly to liberate three hundred maidens kept in slavery in the castle of Pesme Avanture. He reaches the court on the last day afforded the maiden to find a champion. Twice Yvain has promised his aid to maidens in need, and each time another adventure threatens to distract him, but his promise takes precedence. The contrast between these episodes, relating his unwavering fidelity to a cause, and his failure to keep his promise to Laudine points up the moral evolution which makes possible their eventual reconciliation.

I shall later trace the events of these three *romans* in much greater detail, but I think the few suggestions offered here provide ample evidence that Chrétien was systematically exploiting the principle which, through Dante, is known as the *contrappasso*. In these three works he develops the basic pattern: happiness gained, happiness lost, happiness regained. The resolution of this process entails a lengthy process of expiation or retribution, and the hero's offense both necessitates the retribution and determines its exact form.

Cligés, which I shall discuss separately, reflects this pattern even though its use is less precise and simple than in the other works. *Perceval* appears to make extensive use of it, but, as with so many other problems, the unfinished state of this romance obscures the use of *contrappasso* and makes it difficult to define. In a general sense, however, Perceval devotes himself entirely to whatever is related to his conception of chivalry, ignoring all else. In the process, he learns to repress his natural and naive inquisitiveness and other impulses. Consequently, he fails to ask the

question which would have cured the Fisher King. This is the crisis—
or one-half of it, for the same ambition has already caused his mother's
death. To expiate his offense, he must become again what he originally
was, allowing himself to be guided by nature rather than by adherence to
a code, by *nature* rather than *norreture*. Presumably, of course, he will
at the end of the quest have to ask the Grail question, and this fact itself
implies the use of *contrappasso*, although we cannot predict how far it
might go beyond this simple question. In any case, his development will
consist of three steps, extending from the apparently excessive questions
Perceval asked in the initial episode, to his unwillingness (because of the
instruction he has received) to ask the Grail question, to the implied
question which will mark the conclusion of his quest.

In expiating their errors and forging a new identity, Chrétien's
characters do not simply reject the chivalric code as they had earlier
understood it. Rather, they perfect it, fashioning for themselves a personal
ethic which combines the love, devotion, and service which should be their
obligation with the physical and social code which permits them to fulfill
their function. Put differently, Chrétien provides in most of his poems a
development which we may think of as his chivalric dialectic, a dialectic of
thesis, antithesis, and synthesis. We have already dealt with the first two
elements of this dialectic; that is, with a certain attitude or action which is
shown to be flawed and the reaction to it, the opposite attitude or action,
which serves as the expiation of the former. But this reaction is never a
conclusion; it is simply a further step toward a conclusion. If Erec chooses
love and inactivity over normal chivalric endeavor and then reacts against
his choice with excessive activity, he must nevertheless take the third step
and forge from this dichotomy a synthesis of the positive aspects of both
alternatives. In Erec and Yvain the dichotomy is, in over-simplified form,
love/prowess. The synthesis in both is prowess at the service of love—
and justified by love. They do not sacrifice the active life; they *use* it,
but with its self-centered nature modified. This final step restores the
instrumentality of prowess—and it is a step which Gauvain will never
understand. Regardless of the number of knights he defeats or the
number of maidens he rescues—or captivates—the person for whom he
performs such actions is himself.

Even though *Lancelot* develops a genuine contrast between love and
prowess, the conclusion is not unlike that of *Erec*. Lancelot's honor and
fame were of greatest importance to him, and he is reconciled with
Guenevere only after he has learned the relative importance of prowess,
which is without meaning if it is not related to love and service. This work
is complicated by the fact that these two ideals do not achieve equality,

as they appear to do in *Erec,* but the poem does nonetheless redefine chivalry in terms of devotion to something outside itself. The same redefinition occurs in *Perceval,* whose hero finally announces his intention to dedicate himself to a cause other than his own chivalric pursuits. In a passage beginning with the most significant line of the poem,

> . . . Perchevax redist tout el:
> Qu'il ne gerra en un hostel
> Deus nuis en trestot son eage,
> Ne n'orra d'estrange passage
> Noveles que passer n'i aille,
> Ne de chevalier qui miex vaille
> Qu'autres chevaliers ne que dui
> Qu'il ne s'aille combatre a lui,
> Tant que il del graal savra
> Cui l'en en sert, et qu'il avra
> La lance qui saine trovee
> Et que la veritez provee
> Li ert dite por qu'ele saine;
> Ja nel laira por nule paine.

(vss. 4727-40)

Thus, Chrétien's naive hero has learned, at long last, that chivalry is a means rather than an end, that it is in fact good for something.

Most of my comments thus far have excluded *Cligés*—the only one of the five romances in which the hero does not embark on a quest to achieve a goal, rescue a person, or expiate an error. There is, as I have suggested, an impasse rather than the kind of crisis faced by the heroes of the other romances. Cligés finds himself torn not between love and prowess, between self and other, but simply between the love he experiences and the external obstacles opposing that love. The problem facing him is simply to remove the obstacles or to find a way to circumvent them.

But the poem does present a variation of the same "before" and "after" pattern we have seen elsewhere: here the division is not a crisis in the hero's life but rather the point at which Alexandre's story ends and Cligés's begins. For the second half of the work is opposed, not only in a general way, but almost episode by episode, to the first. And specifically the character of the father is opposed to that of the son. Alexandre is reticent; he experiences love but admits it neither to himself nor to others. Soredamors reacts in a similar way, suffering as a result of repressed love. In the second part of the work, Cligés and Fénice have no desire to flee love; they recognize and accept it readily, but their relationship is frustrated simply by the fact that she is married to his uncle. In giving us the story of the father before that of the son, Chrétien gives us the thesis and the antithesis: Alexandre serves implicitly as a negative model for his son. The solution to the lovers' dilemma will not be long in coming, but like most aspects of this work, it will be ironic. The former generation had concealed their love; the younger one had accepted theirs but had secrecy forced upon them. They solve their problem and indulge their love by concealing Fénice's very existence from the world—a specious but effective solution.

Arthur and his court are geographically distant for much of this work, but in other ways they are very much present and of great importance. Both Alexandre and Cligés make pilgrimages to the court. Both are eager to prove themselves there, for they accept Arthur's court as the standard by which knights are measured. Both there and in their own land, proper conduct is a constant concern, but Cligés finds himself in conflict less with the forms and precepts of chivalry than with social and political realities. Just as Alexandre was wrong in repressing love, Cligés would err if he chose love without concern for such realities.

In *Cligés* Chrétien has constructed, on the model of the *Tristan* story, a dilemma without an acceptable solution. Cligés and Fénice are at an impasse, and any decision must result either in a perversion of the social order (if the emperor's wife and his nephew avow their love for each other) or personal tragedy (if they do not). Potentially, *Cligés* is Chrétien's most pessimistic work, because the characters appear to have no way out of their difficulty, but such a judgment fails to take into adequate account Chrétien's method and the resources available to him. For the pre-posterous solution proposed by Fénice and accepted enthusiastically by Cligés does prove to be temporarily (and after other complications, ultimately) satisfactory. But this conclusion is enacted in a climate of such prevarication on their part and irony on Chrétien's that finally optimism and pessimism, acceptance and rejection, success and failure are meaning-less. In the equivocal conclusion, the demands of a social code have ceased to be in conflict with the demands of love. The synthesis which represents a hero's triumph in the other romances is burlesqued in this one: it is not the result of a matured understanding or character but of a stratagem, not a culmination but a *pis aller*, not a refinement of the concept of chivalry but an adept manoeuvre to avoid what cannot be resolved.

Cligés is in search of a solution; Chrétien's other heroes are characters in search of a meaning. Until the crisis, they generally have no purpose (preferring diversion, whether it be in tourneys or in bed) and no identity, as witness the anonymity long maintained by certain of them (Lancelot is unnamed until the middle of the poem, and Perceval refers to himself as *Biax Fix*). Their awareness of their mission and of themselves comes with the crisis, and the remainder of the work recounts their quest for such a meaning—a meaning which gives shape to their adventures and purpose to their lives and which illuminates the nature of love and the proper uses of chivalry. The relationship of male to female and that of the individual to society assume obvious importance in these works, but primary emphasis remains on a character's discovery and renewal of himself.

CHAPTER II

THE CHARACTERS AND THEIR WORLD

Objects and Symbols

Chrétien's works present a fictional universe which is fully furnished and which is frequently described to us in realistic and vivid detail. While Chrétien sometimes contents himself with a brief reference or an aside assuring his reader that further detail is unnecessary, he has at other times recourse to a descriptive method which is concrete in nature and visual in perspective. When Perceval, for example, approaches the castle of Gornemanz, Chrétien offers us minute detail on its appearance, even though there is little more than its fine workmanship and imposing situation to distinguish it from any other castle. Moreover, we follow Perceval closely as he nears the castle, passes by a smooth rock, turns left, takes in the view, and approaches the bridge. While Chrétien's contemporaries may not have needed a description of a castle, Perceval certainly did, and each new experience for him is presented to us with the same systematic and thorough accumulation of detail with which he must have catalogued it in his own mind; just as "knight" was for him a word which designated a person properly accoutered with helmet, hauberk, sword and lance, so is a castle apparently a combination of imposing walls, towers, gates, and bridges:

> Et vit les tors de[l] chastel nestre,
> Qu'avis li fu qu'eles naissoient
> Et que fors de la roche issoient.
> Enmi le chastel en estant
> Ot une tor et fort et grant;
> Une barbacane molt fort
> Avoit tornee vers le gort,
> Qui a la mer se combatoit,
> Et la mers au pié li batoit.
> A quatre parties del mur,
> Dont li quarrel estoient dur,
> Avoit quatre basses torneles
> Qui molt estoient fors et beles.
> Li chastiax fu molt bien seans
> Et bien aesiez par dedans.
> Devant le chastelet roont
> Ot sor l'iaue drecié un pont
> De pierre, d'araine, de caus;

Li pons estoit et fors et haus,
A batailles estoit entor.
Enmi le pont [ot] une tour,
Et devant un pont torneïs . . . .

(vss. 1326-47)

As this passage indicates, many of Chrétien's descriptions are firmly grounded in concrete reality. The evocation, if not of a castle, at least of strange beasts, unusual bridges, and of course the marvelous color and detail of dress, armor, pageantry, and war must certainly have delighted and enthralled medieval readers; but Chrétien's descriptive technique frequently bears a definite relationship to his literary psychology and to his narrative point of view. In the excerpt given here the detail functions as an indication of the way Perceval perceives and understands the world around him. The world is filled with all manner of objects and symbols, which Perceval, among others, systematically dissects and in many cases misapprehends.

The title I have given to this section (objects and symbols) is, at least in theory, redundant, because in the medieval world, an object *is* a symbol or sign. That is, an object has no meaning in and of itself; it derives whatever meaning it may possess from its use or function. Its meaning is always *potential*, and is related to ideals or experiences. As John Stevens has noted in *Medieval Romance*, things are important in the degree to which they lead us beyond themselves to the perception of a higher reality. Discussing Marie de France and Chrétien, Stevens treats the central image or symbol used by each as "an emphatically realized visual object which points beyond itself," and which ". . . is felt to crystallize the meaning of the scene."[1] But a character who is incapable of understanding that the meaning of an object is potential would no doubt remain unaware of the precise and elaborate organization of the medieval world; his universe would be chaos. And such a comment must immediately draw our attention once again to Perceval. Chrétien's other characters would find themselves in the same predicament as he, were it not that the Arthurian court, with its appealing—but deceptive—organization, appears to offer to them all a meaning and an alternative to chaos. Their error may be no less significant than Perceval's, but we meet him before he has fallen under the Arthurian spell, and without the experience and sophistication already possessed by the others, he sees everything in fragmented fashion. Just as a castle is an assemblage of towers and drawbridges, and just as a knight is but the possessor of armor and weapons, so, to him, is a grail, however beautiful and luminous, an ordinary dish.[2] It excites his curiosity, but no more so than the knights' armor in his mother's forest. For others, the Grail is a proper noun; for him, it is both a common noun and a generic designation: *un graal* (vs. 3220). For him, a symbol remains an object.[3]

Chrétien's symbology is highly developed and frequently subtle,[4] but in the last three romances, it is characterized particularly by the use of one major and central symbol, an object intimately associated with the hero's identity and the story's meaning. In the last work, of course, the symbolism of the Grail permeates the poem.[5] It is related to fertility, abundance, and life, and Perceval's failure to ask the proper question and heal the Fisher King and revitalize his land is itself a symbolic depiction of the inadequacy of the chivalric code as he had accepted it and of the necessity for that code to be completed, if not replaced, by individual and personal acts of charity. The Grail thus serves as the instrument of Perceval's undoing, and it will become the image which inspires him and drives him to undertake the quest. By implication, his compulsion to rectify his fault and to achieve the proper restoration of the Fisher King's health and land points to his need to restore himself and to perfect his character and his code.

Two additional points might usefully be made here. First, the Grail is a particularly intriguing symbol not simply because of the rich and sumptuous imagery with which it is presented, but because when the Grail secret is revealed we learn that the Grail itself—the object—is of secondary importance in the story. It does possess wondrous powers, or, more precisely, it contains an object—the host—which possesses those powers. Yet, the Grail is not even the intended object of the "Grail question"; rather, Perceval should inquire about the identity of the person *served by it*. And, in fact, both of these matters are less important than the act of asking the question itself. Thus, the symbolism of the Grail is progressively displaced from the object toward its effect and ultimately to a person's reaction to it. The movement coincides with Perceval's development from a fascination with objects to a gradual comprehension of their function.

Secondly, it should be noted that the ambiguity of the Grail's symbolic meaning is reflected in the ambiguous effect of the question. That is, there is a kind of symbolic identity of Perceval with the Fisher King: neither of them is whole, and the question which will cure and restore the King will also mark the culmination of Perceval's development. Once again, the hero is both subject and object of his quest.

The cart which delivers Lancelot to Guenevere (and to disgrace and rejection) is a symbol which lacks significant religious overtones[6] but which possesses some of the same social and political implications as the Grail: the heroes' comportment in regard to them illustrates the inadequacy of chivalric endeavor divorced from the ideal of service. The meaning and function of the cart present no great problem of interpretation, but it is nonetheless a symbol of some functional complexity, simply because, with the exception of the queen, all the characters (including Lancelot) misunderstand its significance. More precisely, it has two contrary meanings. Symbols are by nature ambiguous, but this one is explicitly so: in its social context it represents shame, criminality, and disgrace, while the courtly context superimposed over the social transforms it into its opposite—a symbol (whether ironic or not) of love and devotion. Both cart and Grail have symbolic relationships to the social and chivalric codes, but in both works, the hero must subordinate the demands of those codes to the demands of another one. For Lancelot the solution is unquestioning obedience to the lady; for Perceval it is unselfish adherence to a higher moral ideal.

Other than the Grail, which owes its appeal to its symbolic richness (and perhaps to the unfinished state of the poem, not to mention a possible measure of "deliberate mystification" on Chrétien's part[7]), the most striking symbol created by Chrétien is probably Yvain's lion. It is in this symbol and this work that the poet, perhaps more even than in the story of the Grail, found the happy combination of a symbol which could entertain and fascinate the most casual of readers and at the same time translate and crystallize with great precision the meaning of his work. Consequently, a somewhat extended discussion of the lion may be useful in an attempt to define Chrétien's symbolism, which, at its best here, retains its picturesque appeal while achieving a remarkable degree of elegance and artistic effectiveness.

The problem of the lion's meaning in *Yvain* has elicited a number of interpretations, from Gaston Paris's notion that it served no purpose at all to later suggestions that it served as a symbol of *courtoisie* or a representation of all of Yvain's opponents.[8] Perhaps the best known interpretation was offered, in 1949, by Julian Harris, who advanced the argument that this lion is a symbol of Christ.[9] First of all, that was the common symbolic meaning of the lion in the medieval bestiaries.[10] Moreover, as Harris points out, Yvain or someone else invokes the aid of God in each of the hero's combats after this episode. The conclusion is that Yvain is at last admitting the inadequacy of his mortal powers and his consequent need for aid from a higher source—aid provided by the lion, representing grace freely given. We are thus witnessing the transformation of the perfect worldly knight into a highly religious knight, or of a courtly ethic into a religious one.

As provocative as Professor Harris's interpretation is, it nonetheless presents certain problems. For example, Yvain earns the animal's gratitude by saving his life, and we hardly expect to find Christ helping the hero because of a debt of gratitude. In addition, on more than one occasion, Yvain sends the lion aside, and he even beats the animal in an attempt to insure that he will not intrude in the battle (see esp. vss. 4532-36). Does Yvain not want or need God's help during these times? On the contrary, Harris explains that ". . . Yvain obviously has such faith that God will come to his aid that he is sure to win, come what may" (p. 1159). The conclusion is curious: Yvain has such faith in God's aid that he excludes the symbol of that aid from those situations in which he most needs it.

It cannot be denied that the lion commonly represented Christ for the medieval reader, but to assume that it necessarily did in every case is to ascribe to medieval symbolism a rigidity which it clearly did not possess. A particular allegorical system may consist of a number of one-to-one correspondences; symbolism is less restrictive and therefore richer. As Morton Bloomfield has remarked, the symbolic meanings of objects are frequently multiple and even contradictory, and a symbol must be interpreted in its specific context.[11] Unlike Harris, however, I do not see the context of *Yvain* as religious. Yvain's evolution is undeniable, but it seems to me to be a psychological and moral development, with only the religious overtones which we would expect in the story of such a knight, who quite naturally serves God and the cause of right at the same time as he serves his lady and others in need. Both the lion's actions and the structure and development of the work suggest a symbolic relationship between the animal and the moral (but not religious) ideal pursued by Yvain after his crisis.

The lion's symbolic function stands in direct opposition to Gauvain's. Early in the work, Chrétien takes care to establish in our minds a parallel between Yvain and Gauvain. Yvain is the hero of the work and the knight who can avenge Calogrenant's defeat at the fountain, and Laudine marries him when Lunete convinces her that he who killed her husband must logically be the better man of the two. Gauvain, on the other hand, is presented as the epitome of knighthood, and Chrétien says of him:

Cil qui des chevaliers fu sire
Et qui sor toz fu reclamez
Doit bien estre solauz clamez.
Por mon seignor Gauvain le di,
Que de lui est tot autresi

Chevalerie anluminee,
Come solauz la matinee
Oevre ses rais, et clarté rant
Par toz les leus ou il s'espant.

(vss. 2402-10)

The parallel between the two knights is carried to greater length in the
scene of the wedding feast; as Yvain has promised himself to Laudine, so
Gauvain assures Lunete that he will be her knight, to come to her aid
whenever she needs him. Finally, it is Gauvain who persuades his friend to
leave with him to look for adventure, telling him that a knight should not
cease to exercise his prowess just because he has given his love to a lady.
During this entire section of the work, and particularly during the year's
leave which Yvain takes from his wife, the two knights represent the same
ideals—the exercise of valor and the pursuit of adventure for its own
sake.

As long as the two remain together, there is little difference in their
character. Soon, however, Yvain begins to distinguish himself from his
friend, and Chrétien marks this divergence by separating them physically
and recounting henceforth the adventures of Yvain, making only periodic
references to Gauvain. Yvain's evolution begins immediately after his
folie. He is no less valiant after this incident; if anything his valor is
increased. But the significant fact is that his strength and courage are now
put to the service of others, and particularly of maidens in distress
(vss. 4819-20), whereas Gauvain continues to think only of the thrill that
adventure will bring him. The latter is not to be found when he is needed
by those to whom he owes allegiance—first Lunete and later his own
nephews and niece. In each of these instances Yvain comes to the aid of
those in need. He continues to do so and thus develops until he is worthy
of Laudine's forgiveness. At this point he stands in strong contrast to
Gauvain. This, then, is Gauvain's role in the work; he is at first morally
indistinguishable from Yvain, and, since he undergoes no evolution, he
remains for the reader a figure of what Yvain once was—a knight who
sought adventure for its own sake, with little consideration of his
obligations. Gauvain is no less a symbol than the lion. Yvain does evolve,
of course, and we see the emergence not so much of a religious ideal as
of a new ideal of knighthood, the principles of which are responsibility
and service.

Shortly after Gauvain leaves the scene the lion appears, and from that
point on it is the animal, rather than Gauvain, which we see with Yvain.[12]
Thus, the hero simply exchanges one companion for another, and having

noted the symbolic relationship between Gauvain and Yvain, we may reasonably seek a relationship of a similar nature between Yvain and the lion.

In any consideration of the animal's role, we should take into account not only the usual beliefs about lions (as Harris has done), but also the characteristics peculiar to this one: his gratitude, devotion, and service to his master. For it is important to keep in mind that we are dealing not simply with a lion, but specifically with a *tamed* lion. This, it seems to me, is the key to the understanding of his basic role. A reader might well associate a lion either with Gauvain or with Yvain, for all three embody certain virtues, principally courage and strength. But if a lion is emblematic of courage and strength, then a *tamed* lion must suggest those traits subdued or, more precisely, put to use in the service of one who needs aid. And once this dimension is added to what we know of the lion, the identification with Gauvain is no longer possible, while that with Yvain is strengthened. For the lion represents not only courage and strength but also the ideals of devotion and service, ideals generally foreign to Gauvain but now actively pursued by the hero.

Like Gauvain, Yvain had first considered adventure a value and an end in itself, whereas he has now come to understand that, instead of leaving others to seek the thrill of adventure, he must undertake adventure precisely in order to serve others. The lion's constancy is evidence that the quest for adventure is not incompatible with devotion to a single person, as Gauvain had led his friend to believe. Yvain must now work to make himself worthy of Laudine's love, and from this point on he cannot pause in his search for a new reputation and identity. That this identity is symbolized by the lion is made evident not only by the hero's literal association with the animal, but also by the very name by which he wishes henceforth to be known—*le Chevalier au lion*. The name is not casually chosen; during the second half of the romance, Yvain puts himself at the service of others, just as the lion at the same time puts himself in Yvain's service. The lion must then be the personification of his master's new purpose and resolve.

Thus, Gauvain and the lion can be seen as symbolic opposites, insofar as the former represents adventure for its own sake, and the latter, responsible adventure, or adventure undertaken in the service of others. As Yvain progresses temporally through the work, he also progresses from an identification with Gauvain to an identification with the ideal which the lion represents.[13]

As we read descriptions of the lion in the bestiaries, it is not difficult to understand why it could symbolize Christ, for the king of beasts quite logically represents the king of men. It is the strongest, noblest, and most courageous of beasts. These are the features which make it a symbol of Christ; why do they not at the same time make it an apt figure of the knight, who sought to distinguish himself by strength, nobility, and courage? It is difficult to imagine that such an interpretation should not occur to a medieval reader of chivalric romances. But the essential point is that this particular lion corresponds not to what Gauvain was, but to what Yvain has become.

It would of course be altogether possible for a particular reader, medieval or modern, to consider the lion as a religious symbol, for literary interpretation is a highly personal enterprise. Moreover, the interpretation suggested by the bestiaries illustrates a significant characteristic of medieval symbolism, which we might call resonance and which consists of a series of echos set up by a symbol. That is, the symbol has the power to evoke many subsidiary interpretations without either imposing or excluding certain of them; symbolism is expansive instead of exclusive. In the case of Yvain, we find numerous details which suggest that he himself becomes like Christ—but the key word here is "like": he is Christ-*like* but he is not Christ; he is a figure, but not a symbol, of Christ.[14] This figuring effect, instead of bestowing divinity on him, simply enhances his stature as a devoted knight and servant. If his evolution is primarily moral, rather than religious, then the lion should be seen first as a projection of Yvain's ideal—responsibility, devotion, and service—in the pursuit of which he performs noble acts (e.g., delivering three hundred maidens from slavery) recounted with extravagant messianic imagery:

Tantost mes sire Yvains s'an torne
Qui el chastel plus ne sejorne,
Et s'en a avoec soi menees
Les cheitives desprisonees;
Et li sires li a bailliees
Povres, et mal apareilliees,
Mes or sont riches, ce lor sanble:
Fors del chastel totes ensanble,
Devant lui, deus et deus s'an issent;
Ne ne cuit pas qu'eles feïssent
Tel joie com eles li font
A celui qui fist tot le mont,
S'il fust venuz de ciel an terre.
Merci et pes li vindrent querre
Totes les genz qui dit li orent

Tant de honte com il plus porent:
Si le vont einsi convoiant.

(vss. 5765-81)

The first two romances of Chrétien do not organize themselves to such an extent around a large central symbol, but the use of objects with important suggestive associations is no less an essential element of Chrétien's compositional technique in those romances than in the later ones. From the white stag to the sparrow hawk to the horn in *Erec*, and from the cup, which is to serve as a prize for a knight, to the golden hair Soredamors sews into a shirt for Cligés's father, and with countless other symbols in all the works, Chrétien uses objects to translate emotions and ideals. Chrétien's is in some ways a highly idealized universe, but in another sense it is quite concrete. One function of his emphasis on *things* is simply to capture that idealized world in specific, realistic visual terms. In other words, objects function, in a sense, as a kind of "objective correlative," permitting Chrétien to convey subtleties and abstractions by means of material representations. The interplay of fantasy and reality in Chrétien's romances and the treatment of psychological, ethical, and moral questions amid a profusion of objects, many of them commonplace, lend clarity to his abstractions while maintaining the appeal of a strong and direct narrative line.

Perception and Illusion

My conclusion to the preceding section offered a technical justification for Chrétien's emphasis on objects, but there is a very reasonable thematic justification as well: his emphasis corresponds to a preoccupation with objects on the part of many of his characters. Those characters are fascinated with the physical world and the things in it, and in many instances their fascination is increased by their tendency to attach implicit value to objects. This is the case, most notably, with Perceval, whose fondest ambition in the opening section of the work is to be the possessor of a suit of armor. That is, just as knights may seek adventure or adhere to their code of conduct without a true understanding of chivalry, they may also value a physical object without the ideal it represents. Perceval mistakes the *signifiant* for the *signifié*, ascribing worth to an object which in reality derives its value only from the validity of what it represents.

Variations of such a concern for objects occur throughout Chrétien's work, and one of the clearest illustrations of such a preoccupation is to be found in *Cligés*. While Perceval values the object without understanding that it has any meaning beyond itself, Alexandre does apparently understand that fact but requires the object as a visual and concrete representation of the meaning. Alexandre, as Peter Haidu has suggested,[15] belongs to a "proto-courtly" generation and grapples poorly with the subtleties of love. Thus, in attempting to express his love abstractly in a monologue, he first transforms the abstraction into a sensual and physical image (Soredamors's body), and then he confuses the soul's window (i.e., the heart) with a mirror (see Haidu, p. 70). His objectification of ideals and emotions takes other forms as well: one of the threads running throughout the first half of the romance is the gold one sewn by Soredamors into Alexandre's shirt. After the shirt is first given to Alexandre, Chrétien makes periodic, almost rhythmic returns to the subject, as its owner presses it to his mouth, constructs monologues around it, and nearly swoons. His rapture, in fact, appears no greater when he is actually in the presence of his beloved. He is forced to think of love, metaphorically, in terms of emblems, of things. Not only does he require a symbol of his love, but he identifies the symbol with what it denotes—and in his monologues he awkwardly distorts the precise relationship of that symbol to the reality.[16]

The relationship of the physical to the non-physical (of the object to its meaning) presents difficulties for a number of Chrétien's characters, and Chrétien's exposition of such problems quite naturally includes an emphasis on the thematically inseparable subjects of physical perception and psychological or moral vision. The physical aspect of perception is one of the nearly constant themes running through his romances. Those works are populated by characters who are constantly watching others and being watched by them, and instead of telling us that a knight (or, in the following example, a horse) approached, Chrétien will usually tell us that someone *saw* him approach:

> . . . . issir an voient
> Le cheval Kex, sel reconurent,
> Et virent que les regnes furent
> Del frain ronpues anbedeus.
>
> (*Charrette*, vss. 258-61)

One passage of only about one hundred lines in the *Charrette* contains over twenty references to sight (vss. 4737-4835), and such passages are far from rare in Chrétien's work.

This theme has occasioned brief commentary,[17] but its precise function in the romances has not been adequately defined. The emphasis on perception is of course in the interest of simple narrative effectiveness—always a concern for Chrétien, who consistently chooses to depict or dramatize events, rather than describe them (in Henry James's terms, Chrétien is "showing" instead of "telling"). In some instances, moreover, there is a relationship between the author's technique and a particular character's perception, as I have suggested in regard to Perceval. For him, the world is filled with discrete objects and details, with phenomena, but until his progressive enlightenment after the Grail Castle scene, they are not integrated into a system and they remain without real meaning; in a cliché worthy of Perceval himself, he is unable to see the forest for the trees. And Chrétien presents the world to us in precisely the way Perceval perceives it. In *Erec et Enide*, to offer another brief example, when groups of knights repeatedly attack Erec, we see the entire scene through Enide's eyes, so that the emphasis in these episodes is less on the danger he faces than on her dilemma and the action she takes in reponse.

In many cases, however, perception itself, the simple act of seeing, is less significant than *faulty* perception or the misinterpretation of perceived phenomena. In such instances, Chrétien is treating one of the most common themes in medieval theology and literature (as well as in the literature of our own period), the opposition of illusion and reality. From the biblical "For now we see through a glass darkly. . ." to the insistence on the illusory nature of worldly happiness, there is no lack of authority for this theme. Chrétien exploits the theme extensively, developing situations in which, in a variety of ways and for a variety of reasons, we observe a discrepancy between reality and a character's perception of it.

Writing on *Cligés*, Peter Haidu comments that "things are rarely what they seem" (p. 82) in this romance. As a matter of fact, the same is true, in greater or lesser degree, of Chrétien's other works; phenomena, in this literary universe, are illusive. It is simple enough to find plays on the descrepancy between appearance (or illusion) and reality throughout the romances. We have only to think of Erec's apparent death, which leads to Enide's proving her love, or of Yvain's invisibility, or of the praise of secret virtue in the prologue to *Perceval*. *Cligés* in particular abounds in hidden identities, just as it does in hidden motives. Cligés long remains anonymous at Arthur's court, revealing his identity only when he is accepted and admired by all. Repeatedly, in this romance, armies or knights hide or disguise themselves, and stand revealed later; in one case (*Cligés*, vss. 1704-10), they are discovered through an act of God, who hates traitors and thus causes the moon to shine and reveal their presence.

If perception plays a somewhat lesser role in *Yvain*, it appears to become almost an obsession with Chrétien in the *Charrette*. There he makes continual reference to sight and even to the angles from which things are seen; the romance turns furthermore on questions of concealment, anonymity and mistaken identity, imprisonment, and false rumors. Not only does the ethos of the *Charrette* differ radically from that which the poet develops elsewhere,[18] but the use of objects differs here as well; while things normally serve as signals, as cues leading to the perception of reality, traditional perceptions are overturned in the *Charrette*, and the cues are thus misleading—for Lancelot and for the narrator. The perceptual problem is thus somewhat different from that of the other romances. Here, as I suggested, a cart used to transport criminals symbolizes love and devotion. We expect knights to embrace the good and shun the bad, and Lancelot is no exception, but the value judgments formed by the other works are not applicable to the *Charrette*. Love transforms values in all the romances, but in this one it inverts them and turns an evil (dishonor and disgrace) into a virtue.

Finally, in *Perceval*, the naive hero undertakes a thorough and systematic exploration of his world, and throughout the work he demonstrates a remarkable ability to misinterpret or misunderstand absolutely everything in it, mistaking knights for devils and angels, and tents for churches. It is Perceval who thus provides the most striking illustration of a knight who commits all the errors possible—errors of perception, of understanding, and of moral conduct. It is he whose vision is most clouded by naiveté, ignorance, and sin; and, interestingly, he is more preoccupied than any other character with physical objects. He both misidentifies objects in his world and misunderstands their function; he long remains entirely incapable of distinguishing symbol from meaning or, in regard to the code of chivalry, *forme* from *fond*. What interests him is form; that is, the physical trappings and the rules of knighthood. His fascination with those trappings blinds him to all else, and his moral blindness, as we have seen elsewhere, leads him inevitably into error.

This brief reference to Perceval (which will be expanded later) brings us back again to our beginning—the crisis. As critics have traditionally pointed out, Chrétien is exploring the relationship of prowess to service and love, and he depicts crises which arise from a faulty notion of this relationship. Thus, the most fundamental failure of Chrétien's characters is less one of perception in a physical sense than of *conception*, of understanding; it is their inability, through ambition, sin, ignorance, or immaturity, to comprehend the dual nature of chivalry and to embrace the complementary virtues of love and prowess. They mistake a valid *part* of it for its whole meaning and purpose, and this illusion, a kind of moral synecdoche, is frequently the source of their crises. The relationship between illusion, misunderstanding, and faulty perception in a physical sense is in some cases less than clear; no *essential* connection exists, particularly between the last two. There is rather a suggestive relationship; although the characters' failings amount to a psychological or moral deficiency, the poet has frequent recourse to its material counterpart. His art usually provides a physical or narrative reflection of the ethical problem being treated, and we may expect him to deal with both literal and figurative aspects of sight. Thus, a character like Perceval, whose moral malformation leads him into error and sin, may be expected to misapprehend and misinterpret the most commonplace of phenomena. The play on perception, understanding, and illusion is a primary source of drama in Chrétien's romances.

Character Drawing

It has been suggested that Chrétien is interested primarily in ideas, rather than in characters and their psychology. As I mentioned in chapter I, he is conducting an extended examination of chivalry and the knight's role in the world. In a sense, we might think of his work as an *essai*, in the etymological sense of the word: Chrétien is "trying out" his ideas by casting them in changing fictional forms and approaching them from different points of view. Commenting that "romance by its very nature favours variety rather than consistency," Eugène Vinaver points out that the author's works ". . . represent varying attitudes to such important 'doctrinal' issues as the courtly code of behavior, the duties of a knight towards his lady and towards knight-errantry, and the duties of the lady herself."[19] Yet, it is also true that the quest was in large part a psychological enterprise,[20] for the crisis necessitates a personal renewal, in which the hero constructs for himself an identity in accord with his expanded or perfected comprehension of his purpose. His adventures thus constitute both a moral and a psychological rebirth. From one point of view (specifically, that one which recognizes Chrétien's work as ficitonal creation rather than social or moral documentation), it is clear that he is interested less in Arthurian society and its limitations than in his characters' reaction to them, less in the problems he poses than in the process by which his characters, with a great deal of anguish and pains-taking effort, forge solutions to those problems. There is thus a definite emphasis on psychology in Chrétien's romances, but in general this emphasis is reserved for the presentation of his primary characters.

It is true that even Chrétien's heroes sometimes act and move like automata, appearing to possess no power of will to do anything but continue their wanderings in search of adventure or expiation. This characteristic, perhaps most notable in *Erec et Enide*, simply demonstrates the obsessive nature of the quest; the crisis forms the hero's resolve but also deprives him of normal reactions. His mind, his nature, his reactions appear to have been suspended—or perhaps "erased" would be a more accurate reference to the *tabula rasa* created by his rejection of everything he has been until that time.

Before and after the quest, however, we usually get to know Chrétien's major characters with a certain degree of familiarity, for they exhibit a fair range of emotions and reactions. Those characters are of course driven by ambition (*Perceval*, vss. 493-95: "Molt m'en iroie volentiers/Au roi qui fait les chevaliers,/Et je irai, cui qu'il em poist"), pride, and an intense concern for reputation (*Yvain*, vss. 4273-75: "Vialt que il soit dit et conté,/Que por neant prant sa bonté/Qui vialt qu'ele ne soit seüe"). Indignation and anger are frequent and natural emotions, since the knight encounters frequent affronts, and he is also capable of experiencing sorrow bordering on despair, when, as in Yvain's case, he must leave his lady or, particularly, when he loses her love.

In none of these cases, except the last one (Yvain's taking leave of his senses), is Chrétien's psychology particularly penetrating, simply because it does not need to be. His art does not require fuller development of psychology, and as a result the characters are generally flat; we see only the traits of character, emotions, and impulses which are pertinent to their situation and story, and such traits are usually communicated to the reader by a word or phrase. This is in no way intended as a suggestion that Chrétien creates "cardboard" figures, which are not the same as flat characters. A number of his creations achieve remarkable vitality despite the fact that we know little of their past and nothing of the incidential aspects of their lives. The use of flat characters, moreover, serves a definite purpose in Chrétien's art, for it focuses concentrated attention on those traits which are important, and it prevents our being distracted by extraneous details.

Chrétien's focus is also selective in another sense. The only character who receives any psychological development is the hero (and, in the first two romances, the heroine). If we leave aside the major characters, we are left with a curiously cold and sterile literary universe. There is no lack of activity; indeed, there is perhaps an excess of it. But the other inhabitants of this universe are functions (or types, or symbols) rather than characters; that is, there is little development of them, and their actions usually take a predictable form. They enter the story when it is their turn, and they leave it when they have played their roles. They function to illuminate the major character, to serve as a model for him, to test him or give him an opportunity to distinguish himself, to announce his errors and spread the news of his successes. Like the presentation of secondary traits, the development of secondary characters is not a requirement of Chrétien's art. It is only the main character who evolves, and it is this evolution taking place in a climate of psychological and moral stasis which gives greater emphasis to the hero and thus justifies Chrétien's perfunctory drawing of secondary characters. The hero moves as a larger-than-life figure in a world where objects and persons come into focus when they come into contact with him, where nothing happens which is not related to him. This is of course true in most fictional art, which is by nature selective; few events occur without motive or meaning. But in the case of Chrétien's works, this selectivity is emphasized to the extent of making the hero the explicit and literal center of the romance universe, a focus which is entirely appropriate to his role, whether it be as hero, lover, or messiah.

Other characters, from Calogrenant to Guenevere to Laudine, may at times be presented, respectively, as ashamed and embarrassed, petulant, and coy, but such an enumeration demonstrates nothing more than the poet's restriction of their emotional range. Simple and constant in emotional composition, such characters tend to be *posited*, and there they stay, in obedient adherence to the role and character assigned them. The few secondary characters who do have sharply defined personalities, who stand out from the rest, are nonetheless as static as the shadowiest inhabitant of Chrétien's universe (only Blancheflor and Lunete present some degree of psychological interest, but still without undergoing any evolution). All these figures are less literary characters in the full sense of the word than silhouettes.

Few of the characters at the court receive any particular attention. Arthur, in *Erec*, proves himself stubborn enough to order the hunt for the white stag even though he knows it will cause disputes among the knights. Otherwise, Chrétien's works present him as a blurred character, who varies from inspiring leader to doddering old man.[21] It is Keu, his seneschal, who stands out with greater relief than anyone else at court. He serves as the repository for more traits and emotions (most of them bad) than any other secondary character. He is, we are told, *ranponeus, fel et poignanz et venimeus* (*Yvain*, vss. 69-70), and these are characteristics which never change. His qualities are amply—and constantly—illustrated, from his belittling Calogrenant (in *Yvain*) to his violence in striking the smiling maiden and kicking the fool into the fire (in *Perceval*).

Gauvain is certainly one of the major characters in Chrétien's work, and he acquires this importance despite his frequent if not habitual absences in situations where his aid is needed. As the exemplar throughout the world of the Arthurian ethic, he exercises considerable influence, serving alternately as a positive and a negative example for the hero. We know all we need to know about him, but that is rather little. His reputation for physical exploits requires no rehearsal here, but if we turn our attention to his psychological construction, we find practically a total vacuum. Impatient and ambitious, proud and somewhat irresponsible, he is little else. He devotes himself readily to a cause and never to a person. The one apparent exception to that statement occurs in *Yvain*, when Gauvain meets Lunete at Yvain's wedding, but even there we find little evidence that he experiences any particular emotion. Unlike Yvain, whose love for Laudine is born in an atmosphere of adoration, fear, hope, and despair, Gauvain experiences few significant emotions. Chrétien does announce that, as Gauvain and Lunete become acquainted, he values and loves her greatly, "et por ce s'amie la clainme" (vs. 2422). Yet he makes such a commitment—and for him any commitment is worthy of note—not for love or inclination, but rather because of his gratitude for her having saved his companion and friend. After his pride, feelings of gratitude and friendship (for Yvain) are the most intense emotions Gauvain is capable of experiencing.

It comes as no surprise that the only emotion that is subjected to any real analysis and depicted in great detail is love. Even the characters' ideas of chivalry and prowess are not developed to the same extent—and for good reason. As I have suggested, the basic problem in most of the romances is the conflict between love, personal inclination, and devotion on one hand, and the social code of chivalry on the other. The latter, the active principle in those works, is a code which is, and remains, external to the characters themselves; the conflict then is between an internal force and an external principle. Furthermore, chivalry, as it is presented in the stories, is a fixed and static force; analysis is unnecessary because change is impossible. But it is love which gives meaning to prowess, and it is the forms and effects of love which thus provide the only extensive material for psychological examination.

The originality of Chrétien's treatment of love lies in the way he relates it to prowess, and not in the emotion itself or its effect on the lovers (from the latter points of view Chrétien is entirely conventional). Lancelot is usually taken by critics as the model of the lover in Chrétien's romances, but I am not convinced that that choice is any more appropriate that would be Erec, Yvain, or perhaps Cligés. Love-sickness afflicts them all; except for Yvain after his departure with Gauvain, their every thought is for their lady. They turn pale in her presence, and they are torn by doubts. In fact, whether Capellanus's intent was serious or ironic, most of his "rules of love" could serve as accurate descriptions of the behavior of Chrétien's lovers.

While the lover's love and fear may reduce him to silence or awkwardness in the presence of his beloved, his casuistic monologues give evidence of an extraordinary gift for *préciosité*. The monologues in *Cligés* are elaborate, lengthy, and (for many tastes, including my own) tedious. They demonstrate in great detail the vacillations, the fear and self-doubts to which the character is subject:

> Donc n'est mervoille, se m'esmai,
> Car molt ai mal, et si ne sai
> Quex max ce est qui me justise,
> Ne sai don la dolors m'est prise.
> Nel sai? Si faz. Jel cuit savoir:
> Cest mal me fet Amors avoir.
> Comant? Set donc Amors mal faire?
> Don n'est il dolz et debonaire?
> Je cuidoie que il eüst
> En Amor rien que boen ne fust,
> Mes je l'ai molt felon trové.

> (*Cligés*, vss. 653-63)

This is Alexandre's speech, but it is less than ideal as an illustration, simply because, either fascinated or confused by the subtlety of his rhetoric, he loses his train of thought and transforms the image of Love's arrow, by which he has been wounded, into a highly sensual image of his beloved's beautiful and desirable body. More to the point are the monologues of Cligés or of Yvain; the latter, especially, illustrates the effects of love both upon the lover's mind and upon his language. As the lover experiences equal measures of fear and hope, and of joy and sorrow, Chrétien develops rhetorical paradoxes to depict love:

> Son cuer a o soi s'anemie,
> S'aimme la rien qui plus le het.
> Bien a vangiee, et si nel set,
> La dame la mort son seignor;
> Vangence en a feite greignor,
> Que ele panre n'an seüst,
> S'Amors vangiee ne l'eüst,
> Qui si dolcemant le requiert
> Que par les ialz el cuer le fiert;
> Et cist cos a plus grant duree
> Que cos de lance ne d'espee:
> Cos d'espee garist ct sainne
> Molt tost, des que mires i painne;
> Et la plaie d'Amors anpire
> Quant ele est plus pres de son mire.

> (*Yvain*, vss. 1364-78)

With desire and despair, Yvain debates his prospects:

> . . . Por fos me puis tenir,
> Quant je vuel ce que ja n'avrai;
>
> . . . .
>
> Qui Amor en gré ne requialt
> Des que ele an tor li l'atret
> Felenie et traïson fet;
> Et je di, qui se vialt si l'oie,
> Que cil n'a droit en nule joie.
> Mes por ce ne perdrai je mie,
> Toz jorz amerai m'anemie,
> Que je ne la doi pas haïr
> Se je ne voel Amor traïr.
> Ce qu'Amors vialt doi je amer.
> Et doit me ele ami clamer?
> Oïl, voir, por ce que je l'aim.
> Et jc m'anemie la claim
> Qu'ele me het, si n'a pas tort,
> Que ce qu'ele amoit li ai mort.
> Donques sui ge ses anemis?
> Nel sui, certes, mes ses amis.

(Yvain, vss. 1432-33, 1448-64)

Chrétien's analyses of love provide much of the interest of his works, but the term "casuistry" refers here both to traditional discussions and debates about love, such as those noted here, and to casuistry of the opposite sort—the characters' ability to convince themselves logically of whatever they already feel, to turn the rhetoric of love or chivalry to their own ends. Again it is *Yvain* which provides the clearest illustration of this fact. After Laudine thinks for a long time about Yvain and imagines a dialogue with him, the birth of her love is recounted thus:

> Ensi par li meïsmes prueve
> Que droit san et reison i trueve
> Qu'an lui haïr n'a ele droit,
> Si an dit ce qu'ele voldroit,
> Et par li meïsmes s'alume.

(Yvain, vss. 1775-79)

Not only Laudine, but Gauvain as well manages to pervert logic for his own uses. He plies Yvain with an argument which, according to all we know about chivalry and according, as well, to what *Erec et Enide* has already demonstrated, is unassailable; but in fact that argument is here turned against love. As a result, Yvain follows his friend's frivolous advice,

leaving his wife and failing to return, thereby committing a nearly un-
pardonable crime. In a world as preoccupied with action as the Arthurian
realm appears to be, words nevertheless play an unusually important role.
Language is doubly related to psychology in these works; it does not
simply depict psychological states and changes, but it functions moreover
as the instrument of such changes. And as Gauvain uses it against Yvain,
it proves to be the knight's most dangerous weapon.

The characters' rhetorical dissection of their feelings and particularly
their capacity for self-doubt and sometimes for self-deception provide
adequate evidence of the importance of psychology in Chrétien's works—
despite the selectivity of his psychological focus and the economy with
which he ordinarily presents his characters' emotions and feelings. As with
every other element of his work, Chrétien's literary psychology is freely
fashioned to his own purposes. He can depict the birth or pain of love in
elaborate detail, or, where such detail is not required, he can pass over a
character's psychological composition with a word or a brief explanation.
The unfolding of his stories seems in many instances to be accomplished
by an almost rhythmic alternation of rapidly developing action (recounted
from a point of view located well outside the story and the characters'
minds) and long, introspective monologues, in which the characters
subject their feelings to the most searching scrutiny. The inconsistency
(or, if that is pejorative, the *freedom*) of Chrétien's approach is a strength
of his art: he uses psychological analysis when he needs it and ignores it
where it would be an encumbrance. When he does offer such an analysis,
it invariably demonstrates his own rhetorical virtuosity, while effectively
conveying the complexity of an emotion. And sometimes, as in the case of
Alexandre's monologue, the analysis reveals to us more than the character
himself understands.

CHAPTER III

THE NARRATOR AND HIS STORY

The Narrator's Role

One of the translators of Chrétien, W. W. Comfort, prefaced his text by an admonition that we should read Chrétien "as a story-teller rather than a poet."[1] Most critics since Comfort would probably take exception to his judgment, for I think there is general agreement that Chrétien is both story-teller *and* poet. The two are scarcely mutually exclusive for any period, and certainly not for the Middle Ages. Art was entertainment in the best sense of the word, and the best story-teller was the one who entertained most artfully. As both poet and story-teller, as consummate craftsman and self-conscious artist, Chrétien emerges as the best writer of fiction of his time.

He was conscious not only of his art but apparently of his reputation as well, and his work is rarely encumbered by false modesty. Indeed, at the very beginning of *Erec*, he announces with some pride that a story which has traditionally been garbled and mutilated will be transformed by his art into a *molt bele conjointure*, which will live in memory until the end of Christendom. While he never defines his term *conjointure*, it is clear that it refers generally to the composition of the poem, to its "putting together," to the conjoining of its parts and elements in such a way that from a flawed or chaotic narrative source (or sources) there emerges an organized and coherent work of art.[2] The creation of such a work not only permits the communication of a meaning, but it itself *becomes* a meaning. In dealing with Chrétien's work, we are entirely justified in speaking of conscious artistry, of the pride of authorship, and of the intrinsic value of the text. Chrétien, in short, "knows what he is about," and he has at his disposal the narrative and rhetorical resources necessary to produce such a *conjointure*. What sets him apart from—and above—most of his poetic contemporaries is not so much the themes and motifs he dramatizes, for we find much the same thing in sources, analogues, and imitations of his work; it is simply his superior mastery of the art of literary composition.

Chrétien is at times one of the most visible and intrusive narrators imaginable. He normally begins by announcing that he is going to tell a story; he offers his name in all five romances, and he prefaces *Cligés* by a list of his previous compositions. Moreover, he frequently interpolates into his works a number of comments on his story and on the writer's craft. Such comments prove far from enlightening as a guide to Chrétien's literary methods, of course, for they are for the most part brief asides occupying a line or two before the author returns to the narrative. Sometimes, he comments that twice-told tales are tiresome (*Erec*, vss. 6272-74; also vss. 6420 ff.), and he insists that brevity and economy are artistic virtues. He may also inform us that he has omitted an important detail (*Cligés*, vss. 4244-45) or that he intends to postpone until later the explanation of a fact or person he has introduced:

Mes une en i ot avoec eles
Don bien vos dirai ça avant
(Cele estoit suer Meleagant)
Mon pansser et m'antencïon;
Mes n'an vuel feire mancïon,
Car n'afiert pas a ma matire
Que ci androit an doie dire,
Ne je ne la vuel boceier
Ne corronpre ne forceier,
Mes mener boen chemin et droit.

(*Charrette*, vss. 6242-51)

Not only do such comments tell us little about the writer's craft, but they would seem in many instances to be distracting and useless intrusions into the narrative. As we are getting caught up in the rush of events, the narrator will insert a directive: we are to take notice of a particular character, who will later turn out to be important. He makes a simple statement to the effect that Cligés gave his heart to Fénice; then he interrupts himself with a quibble: "No, I lie, for no one can give away his heart. I must express it differently" (vss. 2780-82). He continues:

Ne dirai pas si com cil dïent
Qui an un cors deus cuers alïent,
Qu'il n'est voirs, n'estre ne le sanble
Qu'an un cors ait dcus cuers ansanble;
Et s'il pooient assanbler,
Ne porroit il voir resanbler.
Mes s'il vos pleisoit a entandre,
Bien vos ferai le voir antandre,
Comant dui cuer a un se tienent,
Sanz ce qu'ansanble ne parvienent.

(vss. 2783-92)

Such commentary, far from rare in Chrétien's work, might well constitute a serious artistic flaw if he wanted simply to establish reader identification with his characters and story. But in fact, that is not as important as the reader's acceptance of the story as artistic creation and entertainment.

Throughout Chrétien's works, there is a strong feeling of the poems' artifice, of their status as created narratives. Apparently, audiences delighted in authors' descriptions of sumptuous feasts, crowded tourneys, colorful and exotic dress; their delight was certainly no less stimulated by the virtuosity those same authors displayed in the construction of debates on love and duty and by the characters' interior monologues.[3] The fictionality of the work remains apparent at every turn, and despite many realistic details, Chrétien's concern for the "illusion of reality" is subordinated to his regard for the validity or truth (the *potential* reality) of the problems and psychology he deals with.

The narrator, whether "Chrétien" or "je," is a visible and indispensable inhabitant of his own poems. The comment "I will speak no more of this subject" becomes almost a formulaic device signaling a change of scene or point of view, but it also acquires value as a signal of the author's presence. This is not quite the same situation as the traditional poetic "I" of medieval texts, which, as Spitzer notes,[4] was general rather than particular. The traditional "I" was nearer to "we," for the experience of the former was understood to be applicable to that of the reader. That "I" refers to the first-person narrator-character (e.g., Amant in the *Roman de la Rose*) rather than simply to the obtrusive narrator. With Chrétien, the "je" is not necessarily identified with the reader: the persona of Chrétien's narrator remains entirely particular and must remain so as long as the notions of literarity and entertainment are attached to the text. It is "I, Chrétien de Troyes, author or narrator," and it can mean "we" only to the extent that our interpretation is thoroughly directed by him, so that our reading of the text coincides with his.

One of the most significant kinds of intrusions on the narrator's part is his frequent explanation, or warning, of what is to happen later in the story. For example, when Yvain promises to return within a year to Laudine, Chrétien appears in the text to inform us, with ironic uncertainty, that he *thinks* Yvain will forget his promise (vs. 2669; cf. *Perceval*, vss. 3248 ff.). In such a situation, suspense is a virtual impossibility, of course, but the writer of romance appears to have attached relatively little importance to suspense, at least in our sense of the word. The author often sees to it that we know what will happen—that we know more than the character himself, who remains happily ignorant of the crisis before him. What the writer thus creates is not suspense but anticipation, which belongs to an entirely different order of esthetic experience. In a general sense, the highly conventional nature of romance narrative works against suspense. When a character seeks adventure, we do not doubt that he will find it; when he enters a battle, it is highly unusual for him to be defeated.[5]

Audiences apparently wondered less what was going to happen than how and when it would (the "accidents" of narrative), not so much whether he would win the battle but the degree and kind of valor it would require, not whether a quest would succeed but the variety and number of adventures awaiting him on his way. When, in *Yvain*, Chrétien interrupts one adventure to recount another, Frappier remarks that his technique serves to "piquer la curiosité,"[6] and he is clearly right, but I think the audience must have had few doubts that Yvain would return in time to save Lunete; of greater interest is the kind of adventure delaying him, the psychological effect of the delay, and the pressure of time, as he arrives at the very last minute. The dramatic interest of such passages is due to artistic and psychological tensions, but not to suspense.

We are thus partners with the narrator; he not only guides us through his fictional present, but he often tells us as well what will happen later. Both the presence of an intrusive narrator and the sort of dramatic irony sometimes created by his intrusions substantially alter the nature of the "fictional contract" he establishes with us. Indeed, the term "fictional contract" is particularly apt when applied to Chrétien, for our relationship with the narrator requires us to accept the fictionality of the work and to lend ourselves willingly (and consciously) to his illusion; it is not quite the "willing suspension of disbelief," but the ready enjoyment of the fiction, whether credible or not. We can continue to disbelieve in the fantastic elements of the story, but because we are constantly aware of its fictitiousness, unsuspended disbelief remains compatible with drama. Chrétien frequently tells us (as in the prologue to *Perceval*) that he found the story in a book, and such a statement may provide us with a respected source of literary authority and moral truth, but not of historical truth.

The author's presence in his work thus draws our attention to the fact that we are dealing with fiction narrated by a story-teller whose primary objective is to excite and maintain our interest and who does all he can to assure that we see what is important, that we understand its function, and that we read the story as he wants us to. And his practice of calling frequent attention to himself reinforces our awareness of the fictionality of his creation. The comments to the effect that "Now I am going to tell you a story," or that "I have skipped over a detail which I should explain to you," or that "Now I am going to demonstrate this point with the following argument," or, in his simple conclusions, that "The story ends here," are not the clumsy comments of a writer who should have kept his fingers out of his work, but the marks both of authorship and of complicity between a narrator conscious of his craft and a public conscious that his craft could provide them the exciting and effective stories they loved.

Chrétien's boast at the beginning of *Erec* is an important passage for an understanding of his art.[7] The "contract" he establishes with his readers recognizes that he, the author, knows perfectly well what should be narrated and how. We are expected to recognize that fact and be led by the narrator through the story. He will be our Virgil, to explain events and at times to inform us that explanations will come later or not at all, to present us with everything we need to know and to skip over that which is irrelevant. He will serve as narrator, interpreter, and sometime censor. As the following section demonstrates, he may, in specific instances and for specific purposes, adopt an impersonal technique, limit his omniscience, or establish considerable distance between himself and his text (and consequently between it and his audience). But even in these cases we remain aware of the author's presence. His narrative attitude may be impersonal, declining to take sides with or against characters, but he remains there, to direct our literary enterprise and to assure and confirm the validity of his.

Point of View

Defining narrative points of view in medieval literature, and specifically in Chrétien, is not always the simple and straightforward task it might at first appear to be. Medieval authors generally assume great freedom (not to be confused with a lack of narrative sophistication) in regard to their technique, moving into and out of the action and the characters' minds, usually retaining their omniscience throughout. And yet, a writer properly sensitive to the demands of his art will instinctively adopt the techniques and points of view which will most effectively produce the literary response he seeks. Thus, although Chrétien's narrator is normally both obtrusive and omniscient, he not infrequently assumes a certain Socratic ignorance, omitting explanations either of the meaning of certain events or of a particular character's emotions and reactions. It is precisely this technical freedom which gives Chrétien's poems their diversity and consequently prevents our offering generalizations applicable to all of them. The romance form favors diversity not only in thematic matter and the attitude taken toward it (as Vinaver states, *Rise of Romance*, p. 32), but in the point of view chosen to present it. Thus, although there are techniques which certain of Chrétien's works share (and which permit us to relate, as Haidu has done, *Cligés* and *Perceval*[8]), the poems nonetheless are best discussed individually.

Yvain, Chrétien's best constructed poem, is also the most straightforward one in its use of point of view, and as a result it presents few developments which require analysis here. Moreover, while it is not without elements of comedy and irony (both important components of several of Chrétien's romances and involving the narrator's relationship to his text), they are accessory to Chrétien's main tone and purpose, and for the most part the narration is direct and economical, without our being denied access to any knowledge we need to understand psychology and action. We never have to wonder about motivation in this work, unless we find it difficult to understand why Yvain would leave Laudine so soon after the marriage (but Chrétien explains that clearly and thus it is a question of credibility, not of understanding) or why Gauvain would accept a cause he knows to be unjust (that is probably clear enough, too, but it is without real importance in any case). Despite the use of illusion in some local contexts (e.g., Yvain's invisibility), this is the only one of the five romances in which, for the most part, things *are* precisely what they appear to be. Of the five, *Yvain* possesses the greatest clarity of form and construction, and it also presents its material with the greatest clarity and directness of technique and point of view.

On the other hand, *Erec*, the romance which is generally, and justly, considered to be the counterpart of *Yvain* (the opposite face of the coin, as it were), presents a more complex psychological drama, and the points of view by which it is presented are correspondingly more complex. Here, in Chrétien's first Arthurian effort, such drama is at its most intense, and the importance given to the relationships between two characters is greater than that of the ideological questions of duty and proper conduct. That the psychology was as important to Chrétien as it has been to the numerous critics who have dealt with it is suggested by the care and attention with which he fashioned his narrative point of view around his characters' consciousness. For it is with a study of point of view that we may provide the best answer to the persistent question: "Why did Erec treat Enide so harshly?"

Erec (we will recall) overhears Enide lamenting the fact that he remains constantly with her instead of participating in tourneys and other chivalric activities which would maintain and increase his reputation. Admitting that she is right ("—Dame, fet il, droit an eüstes,/Et cil qui m'an blasment ont droit": vss. 2572-73), he commands her to prepare to leave immediately with him; he explains neither what is to happen to her nor the reasons for his command. In fact, although we follow them through a large number of adventures, Erec never explains to Enide, nor Chrétien to us, why he treats her as he does, and this problem, more than any other presented by this poem, has attracted extensive attention and provided us with a number of tentative explanations.

Most critics have suggested that Erec doubts Enide's love and wishes to test her; however, Nitze thought his sovereignty in marriage was at stake, while Z. P. Zaddy refers to his wounded *amour propre*, and William Woods resigns himself to the notion that Erec's motivation is confused and his actions inexplicable.[9] These explanations—Woods's excepted—do not seem to me to be mutually exclusive, and critics have perhaps erred by over-simplifying Erec's obviously complex motivation. Most critics have moreover neglected an important aspect of the work, treating motivation but failing to examine Chrétien's method of presenting it. One obvious reason for the difficulty in defining Erec's motivation is that it is not just *obscure*, but *obscured*. That is, instead of simply failing to clarify the reasons for his conduct, Chrétien systematically withholds comment on this subject, constructing the romance so as to deny us our expected insight into his behavior. Thus, an adequate understanding of this portion of the work depends not only on explicit reference to this behavior but also on the much broader question of Chrétien's narrative technique and point of view.

The tripartite form of the romance is readily apparent to even the most casual of readers. What may have escaped notice is the fact that the movement from one division to the next is accompanied by a change in point of view. The poet uses a shifting center of consciousness; that is, he chooses a particular character and filters most of the narrative through that person, and the person thus used (in Henry James's term, the "reflector") changes from section to section.

Chrétien narrates the story, as is his custom, from a modified omniscient point of view. He appears to have access to all the characters' thoughts. Thus, he can tell us that Gauvain is displeased (vs. 39), that Guenevere wishes to know who the knight and dwarf are (vs. 152), or that she is angry and dismayed (vs. 194). The narrator even leaves Erec once and speaks of what is happening back at Arthur's court. Nonetheless, we have at this point only cursory glimpses into characters other than Erec, and in no case do these insights determine the direction of the external narrative or interfere with its effectiveness. It is clearly through Erec that Chrétien filters most of his narrative in the first third of the poem. Not only is he the character whose progress we follow most closely, but we know his thoughts and intentions. We are told his reactions to the dwarf's insulting the queen, to other knights, and particularly to Enide.

Our knowledge of Enide before her marriage is limited to descriptions of her beauty and wisdom, her father's statements about her, and Erec's reactions. When Erec first sees her, Chrétien devotes some fifty verses to his description of her. He contrasts her poor clothes with her natural beauty:

> . . . sa fille . . . fu vestue
> D'une chemise par panz lee,
> Delïee, blanche et ridee;
> Un blanc cheinse ot vestu desus,
> N'avoit robe ne mains ne plus,
> Et tant estoit li chainses viez
> Que as costez estoit perciez.
>
> . . . .
>
> Plus ot que n'est la flors de lis
> Cler et blanc le front et le vis;
> Sor la color, par grant mervoille,
> D'une fresche color vermoille,
> Que Nature li ot donee,
> Estoit sa face anluminee.
> Si oel si grant clarté randoient
> Que deus estoiles ressanbloient.

(vss. 402-08, 427-34)

Later, when she arrives at court, the same detail is used in the description of the dress given her by the queen; a small excerpt of the passage tells us that her mantel was

> . . . . . . boens et fins:
> Au col avoit deux sebelins,
> Es estaches ot d'or une once;
> D'une part ot une jagonce,
> Et un rubi de l'autre part,
> Plus cler qu'escharbocle qui art;
> La pane fut d'un blanc hermine,
> Onques plus bele ne plus fine
> Ne fu veüe ne trovee;
> La porpre fu molt bien ovree,
> A croisetes totes diverses,
> Yndes et vermoilles et perses,
> Blanches et verz, indes et giaunes.

(vss. 1589-1601)

In strong contrast to this physical description is the almost complete lack of insight into her mind. In a few cases we see physical manifestations of her thought, as she weeps and prays during Erec's battle for the hawk and shows her joy openly when he wins. Chrétien mentions once that she is happy to be betrothed to Erec (vss. 685-86). Nothing more. We do not even know her name (nor, so far as we know, does Erec) until their wedding day. She has scarcely spoken, and her words have never been reported to us. In the first part she is thus little more than an object, although an object amply described.

In the final part of the work the principal focus is once again on Erec. While he seeks the adventure known as the Joy of the Court, Enide is again relegated to the background. We learn that she is sad and distressed, but until the adventure is concluded she remains without speaking. She initiates no action, and in fact Erec leaves her behind to await the outcome of his exploit. Only afterward does she talk with Mabonagrain's mistress.

Between the two parts of the work devoted primarily to Erec, the large middle portion is, by its narrative point of view, Enide's story. When Erec forsakes his chivalric life, Chrétien's center of consciousness shifts abruptly from him to Enide. She in her role suddenly shifts from object to subject; the external descriptions of her cease, but we now begin to follow the course of her thoughts and fears. As she laments the rumors of Erec's sloth, Chrétien readily reveals her mental state, and she pronounces a monologue about these rumors (vss. 2492-2503). This is practically the first time she has spoken, and it is literally the first time Chrétien has quoted her words.

Meanwhile, as Chrétien earlier restricted our view of Enide, he now excludes us from Erec's mind. Erec is constantly present in this part of the poem, and he demands that Enide leave with him. Yet, from that point on, he appears to be a one-dimensional character, whose actions are clearly depicted, but whose psychology remains inaccessible. We now follow the story through Enide's eyes, instead of his. At the same time, the external descriptions previously devoted to Enide are now given to Erec. When she explains the cause of her grief to him, he orders her to make ready to leave immediately. Although dismayed, she follows his instructions without hesitation. Chrétien describes Erec's own preparations in minute detail, beginning as follows:

Erec s'asist de l'autre part
Sor une ymage de liepart,
Qui el tapiz estoit portraite.
Por armer s'atorne et afaite:
Premieremant se fist lacier
Unes chauces de blanc acier,
Un hauberc vest aprés tant chier
Qu'an n'an puet maille detranchier;
Molt estoit riches li haubers
Que an l'androit ne an l'anvers
N'ot tant de fer com une aguille,

N'onques n'i pot coillir reoïlle,
Que toz estoit d'argent feitiz,
De menües mailles tresliz. . . .

                                        (vss. 2629-42)

The description continues in this vein, but while these passages suggest that
Erec is proceeding in a calculated, deliberate manner, they tell us little
else. We learn nothing of his mental state, not even whether he was angry.
In fact, as had earlier been the case with Enide, the very abundance of
physical detail emphasizes by contrast the complete lack of information
about his feelings.

Enide's grief and dismay, on the other hand, are presented as carefully
as was her regret for Erec's sloth. She first thinks he is going to send her
away into exile (vs. 2592), and then when she learns that they are to leave
together, she wonders what his intention is (vss. 2676-77). Erec's father
shares this natural curiosity, and Erec finally replies and explains in detail
how he has planned his journey (vss. 2712-14). The significance of this
scene lies not simply in Erec's reluctance to explain his intentions, but
especially in the fact that Chrétien does not share with us the information
Erec gives to his father. Despite his detailed explanation to his father, all
we are told is that his decision is final, that he will take only his wife, and
that if he is killed he wishes his father to care for her. It is perhaps here that
the author's restriction of point of view is most apparent: Erec is reluctant
to offer explanations, and when he does Chrétien refuses to share them
with the reader.

During the major part of their journey, Erec does battle when
attacked, but otherwise limits himself to commanding Enide to remain
silent and to rebuking her for having warned him of approaching danger.
In the first of two scenes which take place in castles, the proprietor, Count
Galoain, speaks primarily with Enide, as Erec sits silently and unobtrusive-
ly nearby. Throughout much of this scene Erec is asleep; in a later episode
he is unconscious. Even at other times, he acts and moves almost like an
automaton, and we have no information about any of his feelings, except
his determination not to be distracted from his quest. Only toward the end
of the central section of the work does this behavior change, as he takes
pity on a grieving lady and sets out to rescue her husband, Cadoc de
Tabriol, from two giants (vss. 4300 ff.). Here, for the first time since their
departure, he and Enide separate. For the defense of Cadoc and his second
battle with Guivret, he leaves Enide behind, as he will do also in the final
episode of the work, the *Joie de la Cort*. Presumably, he no longer requires
her presence because, as we are now told, he has learned how loyal she is to

him (vss. 3480-81). Even to this point, however, access to his thoughts is rare.

Chrétien's shift in point of view, coinciding as it does with the transition from one section to another, has structural significance, but it also suggests that Chrétien has so composed the poem as to restrict our vision at certain points and to exclude us from understanding what is not understood by his "reflector" (hence, the critical uncertainty about Erec's motivation). The poet has very scrupulously and systematically withheld the hero's thoughts and reactions from us, and consequently the principal focus of this section is *Enide's* psychology. This is not to suggest that his motivation is not a legitimate object of inquiry, but only that it contributes little to the effectiveness of this part of the poem. In fact, the obscurity of his motivation is more important than the motivation itself. For the duration of the quest, the story hinges not on Enide's comprehension of his actions, but on her willingness to obey his commands without understanding the precise reasons for them. Significantly, while she wonders what his intentions are, she never questions the justice of his treatment of her.

Because Chrétien offers us little direct insight into Erec's motivation, our conclusions must be drawn from incidental references, from his actions, and especially from Enide's extensive reflections—which *are* shared with us—on her fault and the reasons for their departure. Lamenting her plight, she says she should have known that he was the best knight in the world (vss. 3104-07). From this it would appear that she too had begun to doubt him, and such a doubt would naturally push Erec to demonstrate his prowess and courage to her as well as to others. Moreover, given Chrétien's usual emphasis (in this work as well as others) on reputation and self-esteem, Erec would reason that if Enide believed the rumors, she would love him less. Gauvain's statement that a lady ". . . n'a pas tort, s'ele despise / Celui qui devient de li pire / El rëaume dom il est sire," is made in *Yvain* (vss. 2498-2500) and not in *Erec*, but it is an attitude common to both works. In Erec's only explicit remark about his motivation, he will later say that he has tested her and knows that she loves him greatly (vss. 5097-98). Enide tells us in addition that she is guilty of pride and presumption (*mon orguel et ma sorcuidance*: vs. 3103). She admits that although the rumors about Erec cause her grief, she grieves even more because she may be blamed for the change in him. Her flaw seems to be that she feels concern more for herself than for her husband. She expiates this fault in part by bearing her treatment patiently and unquestioningly, but—what is more important—when faced with the apparent choice between losing Erec and seeing Erec lose his life, she repeatedly disobeys him and warns him of danger. She thereby proves that his well-being is more important to her than her own.

The quest thus seems to me to have a triple function. It is at the same time a test of her love, punishment for her act of pride, and a re-establishment of his proper chivalric and conjugal role. As she proves her love to be undiminshed, he shows the same to be true of his valor.

Chrétien marks the stages of their evolution by his shifts in point of view. Erec, dominant in the first part of the poem, becomes passive and inactive after his marriage, and Chrétien turns his attention to Enide. Her role is the exact opposite: completely passive at first, she becomes bold enough to speak of his recreance. In the process, she becomes the dominant character and the poet's reflector. There is thus an abrupt inversion of their roles in the central portion of the work, and their proper relationship must be established gradually and with difficulty. This is accomplished during the quest, when toward the end Enide again retreats somewhat into the background, although she does not become the entirely passive object she had been at first. The Joie de la Cort episode underlines Erec's own resumption of his proper role, for he liberates another knight from the passivity which he himself has now rejected. Throughout the poem, Chrétien maintains a narrative equilibrium by devoting extremely detailed descriptive passages to the character whose psychology is obscured. As I have mentioned, these descriptions are of Enide in the first part and of Erec in the second; psychologically, by contrast, Chrétien permits insight into him first and her later. Finally, it may be pointed out parenthetically that the change in roles corresponds to a change in setting. Even after their marriage, Erec remains active while they are at Arthur's court, distinguishing himself in a tourney; his recreance begins only upon their arrival in his own country. After their wandering, his ultimate reaffirmation of his role takes place in a third realm, that of Mabonagrain and his lady.

Here, in the first of Chrétien's five romances, he shows himself to be a self-conscious artist, in complete control not just of language and style, but also of narrative technique and point of view. A shifting viewpoint is one method of controlling the reader's response to the characters and story, and Chrétien uses it here to transfer primary emphasis from Erec's actions to Enide's reactions. As intriguing as we may find the reasons for his conduct, the fact remains that they are not clear precisely because Chrétien chooses not to clarify them. The cause of Erec's behavior is a less fundamental question than its effect (and Enide's reaction to it). Furthermore, Chrétien's purpose here is not so much the creation of narrative suspense as it is the heightening of interest in the characters themselves, and particularly in Enide's psychology.

From his first romance to his second, Chrétien's method and his narrative attitude toward his material change radically. *Cligés* is the first of three romances (including *Lancelot* and *Perceval*) which translate into fictional form an essentially ironic vision of character and event. Peter Haidu has offered a very detailed analysis of *Cligés* and *Perceval*, of the irony and comedy Chrétien develops in their exposition. Commenting on the former work, Haidu states (pp. 9-10):

> Much of the time, this irony had the effect of placing the reader in a privileged position vis-à-vis the story. It revealed aspects of character or situation unknown to one or more characters in the situation—as in dramatic irony. It allowed the reader certain insights into the narrative and the values implied by the narrative which were not available to the characters of the romance. It frequently seemed to range the reader with the author as against the characters, as if Chrétien de Troyes were offering a guided tour through a living laboratory of charming foolishness: with a sideward wink or a meaningful nudge, he would suggest comparisons which both brought together certain aspects of his story and provided the observer with material for instructive meditation. It defined one's relationship to the text, a relationship both sympathetic and reserved; this was not a story to become "involved" in, these were not characters with whom a reader might identify himself; one was to keep one's aesthetic distance.

Haidu's study of *Cligés* contains a useful catalogue and discussion of ironic rhetorical figures which the Middle Ages inherited from classical antiquity. That catalogue alone presents ample historical and literary evidence to justify the recent critical preoccupation with irony in medieval texts. But medieval authors had not only access to the rhetorical resources of irony, but apparently a particular and keen appreciation of its possibilities as well, either as a basic vision and approach or as a simple means of emphasizing and clarifying some event. This latter type of irony concerns us less at present (for it has less to do with narrative point of view), but it is nonetheless a frequent and effective procedure in Chrétien's works.

A rather simple, but nonetheless effective example of irony used for emphasis and clarification is provided by Chrétien's consistent use of Gauvain as a foil for another character. Gauvain's adventures frequently resemble those of the hero, and their roles overlap. The simple juxtaposition of two episodes (which resemble each other in narrative content but differ in the response offered by Gauvain and the hero) emphasizes, more effectively than a simple authorial statement could have done, the inadequacy of Gauvain's traditional chivalric response and the validity of the hero's actions.

More to my present point is the other type of irony, involving the author's vision and presentation of his material and affecting large blocks of narrative (if not the entire work) and the climate in which the story unfolds. Such irony is one of the compositional tools which enable the writer to control reader response to the text; it can evoke playful bemusement, pure comedy, or stern condemnation of the characters and story, but in all these cases it functions by creating psychological, or esthetic, distance between the audience and the text.

Parenthetically, we might note that the nature and construction of the romance as a form favor the use (and, perhaps on occasion, the unintended creation) of irony. It is true that, far more than the epic, the romance establishes temporal links between episodes; the work unfolds in time, and there is a sequential consciousness generated by what I have referred to as the "before" and "after" divisions of the hero's experience; yet, such temporal considerations provide narrative links only in the literal development, on the surface of the text. The essential developments of character and event come from more profound sources, from a level at which both temporal and in some cases causal relations are fragile and obscure.[10] Thus, the romance is constructed by an author who juxtaposes blocks of discrete narrative matter. This juxtaposition of episodes may clarify them, or it may emphasize their differences or constitute an implied critique of one. In fact, this juxtapositive composition, close to the *iunctura* discussed by Douglas Kelly,[11] is no doubt an essential element in the creation of the randomness of the quest.

In *Cligés*, the juxtaposition is of large sections of material, and in particular, it is the whole story of Alexandre, the father, which is contrasted to that of Cligés. Haidu has shown that most episodes in the first half of the narrative have counterparts in the second, and the purpose of such correspondences (like those established between the adventures of Gauvain and, for example, Yvain) is to emphasize the differences either between two generations (the "protocourtly" and the "courtly," in Haidu's words) or simply between two characters of different temperament and psychology.

But even within the second half, Cligés, who presumably profits from the contrast with an earlier generation, does not escape the narrator's irony. Here the distinction, unnecessary in *Yvain* and *Erec*, between author (or implied author) and narrator may prove useful, for the latter presents us with a story of two beautiful young people passionately in love who finally surmount the obstacles confronting them and find true happiness. And yet, the poet uses irony and distance to undermine what his narrator has presented and to prevent our full acceptance of the ostensibly happy solution to the lovers' problems. Haidu (p. 112) points out correctly that the ironic presentation of characters and events never destroys the reader's basic sympathy for them.[12] At the same time, it is clear that this irony also functions as a screen which the poet erects between himself and the text, and consequently between his creation and his reader.

When Chrétien establishes the contrast between the "before" and "after" aspects of a character or between another character and the hero, it is ordinarily to the advantage of the latter. This would appear to be the case with the relationship between the story of Alexandre and Soredamors, on one hand, and of Cligés and Fénice on the other. While the first couple refuses to accept and admit the fact that it is love which torments them, Fénice and Cligés do not hesitate to love each other; they would willingly admit their love *except* for external circumstances. Yet, with circumstances opposing their relationship, they find themselves facing a dilemma which will be solved only when Fénice appears to die and is then resurrected to live with Cligés.

There is clearly a moral problem involved in the development of the story; despite the fact that the love Fénice feels for Cligés is illicit, they finally do triumph, her husband Alis conveniently dies, they are united and, we are told, live happily forever after. It is hardly sufficient to suggest that because Alis violated his oath never to marry, he deserves whatever he gets. Such an explanation may prevent readers from sympathizing with Alis, but it does not avoid the moral problem.

Not only do adultery and deceit lead to a happy ending for the two lovers, but Chrétien frequently defends them in the course of the work. To offer only a few specific examples: Fénice (in a passage which Haidu discusses in detail: pp. 33, 91-97) is called at one point a "moult sainte chose" while she is lying apparently dead from the potion. At another point she is able to offer scriptural evidence (from St. Paul) in support of her proposed course of action.[13] Finally, it should be noted that the suggestive value of her name is not limited to the fact that she will appear to die and will then be revived. Rather, the quite normal interpretation of the phoenix's legendary power as an illustration of Christ's similar resurrection could hardly have escaped medieval readers; thus, another religious dimension is added to the presentation of Fénice's character.

The key to much of this part of the work is to be found in the poet's ironic, often equivocating, treatment of his material. The irony throughout *Cligés* is both verbal and structural, but specifically, it hinges here on the fact that what is presented as a moral dilemma for Fénice turns out to be no more than concern for public opinion. In fact, in a particularly ambiguous line, she insists that people not be able to say of her what was said of Isolde, that two men possessed her body while only one of them had her heart.[14] It would be normal, perhaps, to take this as a desire not to repeat Isolde's sin, but we will later learn that the *sin* bothers her less than the damage her reputation would suffer from it. That is, she apparently does not object to *being* like Isolde, only to people's being able to *say* she is. In fact, she never expresses any significant moral concerns, and under these circumstances, her symbolic association with the phoenix becomes more bitingly ironic than was the name Soredamors for a lady who rejected love. When we also note that Fénice's scriptural authority was a falsification of St. Paul's words, garbled to suit her purposes, we cannot be unaware of a wide discrepancy between the way she wants to be *seen* and the way she *is*.

In fact, she does avoid Isolde's sin, but her solution is scarcely better than that sin. Instead of giving her body to two men, she deceitfully denies it even to her husband; she eventually deceives everyone and loves Cligés anyway, and her and Cligés's actions will finally lead to her husband's death.

Chrétien avoids measuring Fénice's actions against normal standards of morality by the simple device of providing another standard against which they are consistently judged: the story of Tristan and Isolde. Such a device permits Fénice to present herself as noble, principled, and idealistic, when in fact she is the opposite. History has proved this device effective, for many readers and critics have accepted the contention that Chrétien is writing an *anti-Tristan*. Of course, he is doing nothing of the kind: the anti-Tristan ethic is the creation of Fénice, not of Chrétien. Thus, while the equivocating response Cligés and Fénice make to their dilemma cannot be considered moral if measured against absolute standards of conduct, Chrétien uses ironic techniques like those discussed above to insure that these standards are not applicable.

There remains the question of the ending, for despite their scheming and deceit, all turns out well, and in fact they appear to be rewarded for their actions. Such an ending may not be satisfactory if we expect vice to be punished and virtue rewarded. But Chrétien constructs a *deus ex machina* ending more in accord with Fénice's presentation of herself than with the reality beneath her presentation. He even offers, in a line reminiscent of Erec and Enide, the following assessment of their relationship: "De s'amie a feite sa dame,/Car il l'apele amie et dame . . ." (vss. 6633-34). However, the ending deserves another look, for once the intrigue is basically completed, the story rushes to a resolution, as they are discovered and pursued and as her husband dies and they live out their lives in bliss and glory. All these events, along with the justificatory monologue of Jehan, occupy only three hundred lines and give to the ending an entirely artificial rapidity which tends to undermine the ostensibly happy resolution of their difficulties. Moreover, this undermining becomes more obvious when Chrétien remarks that since that day emperors, hearing her story, fear that they will be deceived and keep their own wives carefully guarded, allowing them to be attended only by women and eunuchs. Fénice's concern has consistently been for her reputation: she does not want her illicit love known. Now, although she lives in happiness with Cligés, her fears for her reputation are realized, the story of her love is known, and it causes others to suffer.

Thus, the ending of the work is itself highly ambiguous. There is first of all a systematic discrepancy between preparation and result, between expectation and outcome, so that Fénice, with her concern for her reputation, is "rewarded" by the reputation she seeks to avoid. But on the other hand, this dreaded fate does not detract from the lovers' happiness. The poem, then, has neither a happy nor an unhappy ending, or, more precisely, it has both. This ambivalence is simply the last example of a pattern which had existed throughout the work; at numerous points, and especially at the end, the story doubles back on itself to cancel the morality which it has itself ostensibly developed.

The most important conclusion to be drawn is that Chrétien neither negates nor endorses a real system of moral values in this work. This is normal enough, since the characters themselves had no interest in any moral system; their morality (especially Fénice's) was a purely pragmatic one. This conclusion is particularly interesting for technical reasons: in *Erec* and *Yvain*, Chrétien created an implied author whose views on love, chivalry, and marriage are quite evident (and coincide with those of the narrator). Such is not the case in *Cligés*; despite a number of authorial interventions, we never sense that the implied author is imposing his own ethical convictions. One reason we find the characters sympathetic, in fact, is that their equivocations are *not* played off against unequivocal standards of a narrator. To the extent that Chrétien (as narrator) has a point of view in the work, it conforms to that of his characters. He is simply depicting the attempts of his main character (Fénice) to fashion a pragmatic system of ethics by reaction to another one, equally pragmatic—that of Isolde.

The primary focus of Chrétien's irony in this work is of course the characters themselves. They may be originally the innocent victims of a passion stronger than themselves, and clearly, circumstances militate against their love. But regardless of circumstances, their own response to them is equivocating and unsatisfactory. That response contains a large measure of self-deception, as they see things less than clearly, interpret them incorrectly, and adopt a course of action which we would scarcely expect to solve their problem. Ironically, the solution does prove effective, permitting them to live happily ever after—and, on the other hand, it is at the same time an *ineffective* solution, because the reputation Fénice acquires is just what she had wanted to avoid (see *Cligés*, vss. 6642-64).

The characters and their motives are not the only target of Chrétien's irony, which is directed as well toward individual events and toward the problem treated in the poem. Chrétien uses this irony to establish a distance between himself and his text, and it is this distance, rather than the characters' self-deception, which makes it impossible for us to assign an unambiguous meaning to the poem. The dual resolution of the work could be taken as a suggestion that Fénice's concern for her reputation was always misplaced, that personal happiness during her lifetime should have been more important to her than her reputation after her death, but irony and equivocation are so frequent in this work, not only on her part but on the author's, that such an interpretation is far from obvious. Throughout the work Chrétien has systematically refused to identify himself (his implied author) with the morality endorsed by the characters. It would be dangerous to speculate on his motives and to conclude simply that such identification was ethically unacceptable to him. Certainly courtly literature offers numerous examples of authorial approbation given to adulterous lovers, even to those who accomplish their purposes by using guile and deceit (love not only conquers all, but it may justify all). And it is not easy to determine whether the medieval audience might be disturbed by behavior which violated normal ethical standards. U. T. Holmes, dealing with the probable reactions of twelfth-century audiences to stories of adultery (notably in *Cligés*), insisted that they simply would not have been shocked by such things. But at about the same time, J. C. Payen asserted that "les Tristan en vers ont tout autant inquiété le public médiéval qu'ils l'ont bouleversé."[15]

Such questions are of particular interest here, because both *Cligés* and the following work, the *Charrette*, develop intrigues involving adulterous and politically destructive behavior. Although critics have speculated much more extensively on Chrétien's attitude toward his material in *Lancelot*, that question is pertinent to both poems. But it is a question which cannot be answered without reference to the theoretical

bases of literary ethics and to certain traditional ethical phenomena in
the romance.

Corresponding to the psychological neutrality which I have noted
elsewhere, a certain ethical neutrality attends certain of Chrétien's
characters. This is possible because, to return to Vinaver's contention,
the romance is less concerned with the presentation of solutions than
with the exploration of problems. Specifically, this ethical neutrality is a
function of Chrétien's fictional selectivity, but it is in addition related to
the conventional moral value conferred on the inhabitants of the court.
The Arthurian world would seem to be the most moral of worlds. The
knight is sworn to foster and restore right and good, care for widows,
maidens and orphans, preserve his own honor, and aid anyone he finds in
need. Yet from Geoffrey and Wace on, certain characters and events
appear exempt from these moral precepts. Many Arthurian characters are
simply not judged by usual standards in the works of writers like Chrétien
de Troyes. The king himself—Arthur—becomes a doddering old man,
unable to stay awake, frequently ineffectual, sometimes ridiculous—and
yet he ordinarily escapes criticism and the judgment which we might expect
to fall on him. Despite occasional comments (as when he leaves the group
in *Yvain* and falls asleep in his room), he is treated as the proper patriarch
of his realm, admired and respected, even revered by all.

His seneschal, Keu, as we have seen, is noted for the most consistent
and predictable irascibility in the court, and if he quarrels with everyone
and belittles the best knights, he is generally punished, if at all, with no
more than a mild rebuke, and he never loses his position at court.

In at least one case, at the end of *Yvain*, even that paragon of chivalry,
Gauvain, accepts a cause which is obviously unjust (the defense of the
older daughter of the Seigneur de la Noire Espine), but there is no
suggestion of criticism of his actions by the author. The champion of that
unjust cause is not even punished in the final battle between him and
Yvain, for the battle ends in a draw. In these examples, Chrétien creates
characters who perform actions easily recognized as unpraiseworthy—
and who are nonetheless praised, or at least not punished for their deeds.

As a general matter of literary principle, applicable to medieval as
well as modern literature, morality within a work does not *have* to
correspond to that accepted personally by the readers. The writer
necessarily creates his own closed fictional world, which by definition
functions according to its own "rules." Those rules may, or may not,
coincide with those of the "real world." As Robert Champigny has
commented in *Le Genre romanesque*: "Le principe selon lequel les actes
bons selon telle ou telle règle doivent être récompensés est incompatible

avec les valeurs romanesques. . . ."[16] Consequently, it should—at least in theory—come as no surprise that morality in the fictional world of the romance is not always identified with that taught to medieval Christians. But the primary question here concerns the way a medieval poet *deals with* those situations in which literary and religious ethics do not coincide.

Obviously, each author develops his own response to this problem, but an examination of a large number of texts does permit us to draw a conclusion applicable to most of them: as a general rule, the ethical problem for the medieval writer was less the necessity to avoid dealing with "immoral" situations and characters than *to avoid being identified— as author—with them*. Thus, his task is simply to establish, by whatever means, between himself and his text the distance which will preclude the appearance of endorsement on his part.

In the specific cases of Arthur and certain of his knights, such distance is unnecessary—or perhaps it is more accurate to say that it is inherited from the characters' traditional nature or literary function, which appears to confer on them a meaning independent of their particular actions. The use of characters or situations with a predetermined and accepted ethical value permits the author to develop his story so that moral questions about them do not have to be posed. Thus, when it is taken for granted that Arthur is worthy of veneration, this assumption seems to be able to survive local changes, however marked, in his character or behavior. Similarly, Gauvain plays a relatively constant role in Chrétien's works: he is there to provide a model for the hero—a model to be not only emulated but surpassed. He is thus both venerable and flawed, but it is his symbolic function, rather than his morality, which acquires significance in the romance, and this role apparently exempts him from moral judgment. Thus, even though he may, as in *Yvain*, agree to defend an unjust cause, there is, as I pointed out, nothing in the text to suggest that he is criticized by the author, or that he should be by the audience.

As opposed to such situations, in which tradition appears simply to render the moral question irrelevant, there are others in which a moral problem is in fact treated, but in which the author refuses to interpose an opinion and takes definite steps to preclude, not only moral judgments by the reader, but also his own identification with the story. That is, a writer like Chrétien can, when necessary, adopt an ambivalent stance and disappear behind an equivocal treatment of ethical values. He is thus presenting a situation involving ethical questions, but he is neither proposing nor defending (nor, for that matter, criticizing) the characters' solution to the problem.

We cannot legitimately speculate on the thoughts and purposes of the historical person named Chrétien de Troyes, but analyses of his techniques do permit us to draw certain conclusions about the practical influence of those techniques on our literary response. In *Cligés*, he has constructed thoroughly sympathetic characters without lending his weight as author to an endorsement of their actions. Instead of condemning them, or extending approbation, he simply avoids identification with his narrator. He offers neither affirmation nor rejection of their morality, but a complex system of self-cancelling and mutually cancelling ambiguities and ironies, in which it is finally impossible to discern a moral system.

If, in fact, the medieval author faced an ethical dilemma, *Cligés* and the *Charrette* after it offer Chrétien's most elaborate response to it. How is he to present characters or situations which in the "real world" would be unacceptable to his audience? Part of the answer is implied by that question itself, for it emphasizes that the literary world and the "real" world are separate and distinct realms. Yet, a work like *Cligés* presents us with characters who not only indulge an adulterous love, but who scheme, deceive, and lie in order to do so. And it is at this point that the author or narrator will disappear from the text. The key here is the distance—achieved in a variety of ways—which the author establishes between himself and his text and which prevents our identifying his characters' views with his own. This distance is the most satisfactory artistic alternative to the author's explicit condemnation of his story and his characters.

If the questions of the author's presence in his work and his attitude toward his material are complicated enough in *Cligés*, they are yet moreso in *Lancelot*, but here a good deal of the complication has been provided not only by the text itself but especially by some specific critical assumptions concerning this romance.

Traditionally, it has attracted attention as an apparent example of typically adulterous courtly love, and for that reason it stands well apart from Chrétien's other romances. Recently, however, other aspects of the work have occupied critics. Particularly, it has become apparent that Chrétien at times shows Lancelot in a less than ideal—or idealized— light. Douglas Kelly mentions that the hero frequently appears foolish or ridiculous, but he relates these qualities to traditional depictions of folly in love, and he maintains that they never detract from Lancelot's prestige or valor.[17] Other critics have found irony and humor to be more prominent and significant features of the poem, and the conclusion most often drawn from this discovery is that Chrétien is using that irony and humor to undermine the results of the apparently distasteful task imposed on him by his patroness. Peter Haidu deals extensively with *Cligés* and *Perceval* but excludes *Lancelot* from his study: while recognizing that this last "offered a highly ambiguous hero with occasional ironic and even farcical turns," he considers such touches to be "subversive protests by a writer annoyed at a patroness. . ." (*AEesthetic Distance*, p. 10). Pierre Gallais goes further, asserting that Chrétien is denouncing courtly love as a *danger mortel.*[18] In short, critics appear divided as to whether the work is a "serious" romance with incidental comic and ironic undercurrents or an *ostensibly* serious work whose *real* intent—the author's rejection of its premises—is revealed in a superstructure of ironic comment and dramatization.

The *Charrette* does of course differ in several important ways from Chrétien's other poems. Notably, this is the only one of his works in which there is a *real* conflict between love and prowess. In both *Erec et Enide* and *Yvain*, for example, both heroes neglect one aspect of chivalry in favor of the other, Erec preferring love, Yvain seeking adventure with Gauvain. But the conflict between love and prowess is illusory in both cases, and the heroes come eventually to understand that these two elements of chivalry are complementary virtues. In the *Charrette*, by contrast, these virtues are not balanced: love must rule supreme, with all other elements of the chivalric ideal—valor, adventure, renown—subordinated to it. There is thus a basic dualism, a tension or disharmony, residing within the chivalric ideal as developed in this romance but not in the others. The fact that Lancelot appears frequently ineffectual as a knight is a natural consequence of this disharmony.

One cannot help wondering at this point how our ideas of the *Charrette* might differ if it were the only one of Chrétien's works we possessed. In other words, our interpretation of Chrétien's narrative posture seems to be influenced by our consciousness of the ways this work differs from the others, and notably from *Erec* and *Yvain*. Many interpreters of the *Charrette* keep insufficient distance between themselves and the intentional fallacy, basing their judgment of Chrétien's accomplishment on assumptions concerning what he must have meant or what he did mean in the other romances, on assumptions, for example, that in light of the "theses" developed in the other poems, the *Charrette*'s subordination of prowess to love and the adulterous nature of that love must have been distasteful for Chrétien. As a matter of principle, we cannot judge the narrator or his themes in one poem according to standards borrowed from another. It is common to suppose that, as in the case of the other works, love *should* be in harmony with prowess, but the fact remains that in Lancelot it is not, and there is no reason why it must be unless the author chooses to make it so. That is, as an author does not have to agree with his characters, neither does he have to agree with what he himself has written elsewhere. In some cases the assumptions concerning the poet's attitudes are supported by arguments to the effect that Chrétien, finding his task displeasing, declined to finish the work. The circularity of the implied argument is apparent: Chrétien didn't finish the work because he didn't like it; he *obviously* didn't like it because he didn't bother to finish it. This argument is no more reliable than the preceding one. We have only two legitimate guides to literary meaning: what the work actually says and the narrative method and point of view by which it is presented.

In any case, Lancelot's role and character remain undeniably ambiguous. On the one hand, he is presented as a virtuous and valorous hero, remarkable for his purposeful devotion to his queen and his quest. Yet alongside this depiction of him there is the other: he is often ineffectual in his chivalric pursuits and comical in his romantic agony. For example, challenged at the ford (vss. 738 ff.), Lancelot, the paragon of chivalry, is lost in thought and is easily knocked from his mount, after which he tugs comically at his opponent's leg in an attempt to unhorse him. Later Lancelot swoons over a few of the queeen's hairs left in a comb. At another point, when he thinks Guenevere dead, the clumsiness of his attempt to hang himself with his belt attached to his saddlebow is reminiscent of no one more than Perceval. Indeed, the parallel with Perceval is strengthened by the incident in which Lancelot receives chivalric instruction from a maiden (vss. 3666 ff.), and he repeatedly finds himself in situations in which he is dependent on the aid of women who serve him as guides, tutors, and liberators.

Yet these atypical and frequently comical depictions of a knight do not automatically undermine Chrétien's hero or his ethic. The question is whether, and how, we can determine in regard to any recognizably ambiguous text that one view of character or story is to be taken as the "correct" interpretation. And in the *Charrette* I find little evidence that the narrator means to lend his authority to either position at the expense of the other. For despite the fact that Lancelot is easily led into romantic foolishness, ultimately his true worth as a knight is never diminished (except in the eyes of spectators, about whom I shall have more to say later). The two presentations of the hero—sublime and ridiculous—co-exist in a constant state of ambiguity, which, instead of constituting, as some would have it, a denunciation of *courtoisie*, simply makes it possible to assign either view to the narrator. It has rather the effect of *obscuring* the narrator's point of view, of disengaging him from his text. As such, it serves as a distancing technique fully as accomplished and effective as those Chrétien used elsewhere. The chivalric ideal developed in this work and pursued by Lancelot is the subordination of all thoughts and enterprises, of pride and prowess, to love. This view of love and chivalry is unlike that developed elsewhere by the author, but whether he endorses or subverts it cannot be deduced from the theme or character, and to exclude either interpretation we would have to ignore Chrétien's narrative procedure.

If we turn our attention from what is presented to the way it is done, we find that Chrétien's method and the tone of his work are established even before we meet his hero; that is, in the prologue itself. Beginning in an entirely traditional way, he refers to his patroness while denying that he intends to praise and flatter her. But then the prologue takes an unexpected turn, as he begins to do precisely what he has said he would not do. In rather free paraphrase, he says: "No flattery is intended here; some would say that Marie surpasses all other ladies . . . but I am not the kind to flatter my lady . . . Shall I speak of her worth? No, I won't— but it *is* true in spite of me!" (see vss. 1-20).

This is the prologue which Holmes thought carried "a strong note of sincerity."[19] If by that term we mean, as we must in criticism, a persuasive presentation of a narrator's view, then the prologue could hardly be *less* sincere. For here we have the presentation not of one view but of two, which repeatedly cancel each other. Denials, almost self-righteous in tone, that Chrétien is flattering Marie are followed by transparent flattery. His dialogue with himself obscures his authorial intention; that is, the result of this equivocal prologue is the narrator's further withdrawal from his work, and our own distance from the text should increase with his.[20]

The prologue is necessarily a personal document, but the narrative stances are rendered unclear in it simply by the fact of being multiple. This interplay of disparities, begun in the prologue, continues throughout the poem, particularly, as we have seen, in the ambiguous role and character of Lancelot himself. But not only is he shown as both valiant and farcical (a disparity hardly uncommon to stricken literary lovers everywhere); there is a further ambiguity developed in his dual role as questing lover and messianic liberator (although a liberator who must himself be repeatedly liberated by women in order to fulfill his destiny). Foremost in Lancelot's own mind, of course, is the love drama and the quest he embarks on to rescue Guenevere. Except for his hesitation before the cart, he never waivers in this quest, but as it proceeds, he gradually transcends the traditional chivalric role to assume a decidedly messianic character. More and more frequent reference is made to the fact that he is to be the savior, leading the people and freeing the captives in Gorre.

Thus, arriving at a cemetery, he effortlessly lifts the cover of the tomb reserved for him as liberator (vss. 1910 ff.); then, periodically, other characters remark that a savior is coming for the captives, but ironically, Lancelot appears scarcely to be aware of his messianic function, as he thinks only of his love. Even when he does finally liberate the prisoners, this grand event is recounted in rather brief fashion (vss. 3899 ff.) to make way for Lancelot's anticipated reunion with the queen.

Ironic techniques such as those exploited by Chrétien can have the effect of identifying the narrator (subversively, as Haidu suggests) with a position contrary to the one he ostensibly takes, or then can instead have the effect of precluding authorial involvement and preventing our full acceptance of his story and characters. That the latter is the case here—that we are dealing with distance rather than subversion—is suggested by Chrétien's systematic use of another ironic technique to contribute to the narrator's disappearance. When a narrator sees and describes events himself we accept or reject his words by judging whether his views are reliable. But in this romance Chrétien consistently declines to serve as observer, choosing rather to filter the narration through the eyes and minds of others. Consequently, although the author frequently comments on his text, the *Charrette* remains among the most impersonal of his works. The natural distance created by the multiple ironies of the poem, by the ambiguous prologue, and by the frequent comic relief is supported strongly by Chrétien's insistent disengagement, as narrator, from his text.

I have already commented on the visual aspects of the *Charrette*; a perusal of a few pages would suffice to demonstrate the prominence of the visual in the poem. The acts of seeing and being seen, the angle of vision, the concealment from view—all are important and are continually emphasized in this romance. But most significant is the fact that throughout the poem the other characters, and not the author, serve as the observers. This technique might be considered to function simply as a way of rendering the story more vivid and immediate, were it not that, like Perceval in the later romance, these characters systematically misunderstand or misinterpret phenomena. The most striking instance is the recurrence throughout the work of scenes in which Lancelot is condemned as ignoble for having accepted the invitation to ride in the cart. The people observing him judge him by conventional standards, according to which all those who ride in such carts indicate thereby their criminality or ignoble character. In the *Charrette*, however, such conventional perceptions are overturned in favor of others peculiar to this romance. Specifically, it is love which invalidates such perceptions:

the knight who rides in such a cart in obedience to the dictates of love proves not his baseness but his basic nobility.

Other episodes abound in which characters observe scenes and systematically misinterpret them. Ironically, the people who watch from a distance and observe that a battle does not take place between Lancelot and another knight conclude that the latter was intimidated by the hero's stature; in fact, his adversary's father had forestalled the conflict. In equally ironic fashion, those who observe the blood on Guenevere's sheets after she has received Lancelot's visit suspect her of dalliance but suppose the deed to have been done by Keu. Examples need not be multiplied, though we might recall such scenes, involving either physical or psychological perception, as those in which Lancelot thinks the lady with whom he is to sleep has been abducted, in which false rumors are rampant, in which the lions seen at the opposite end of the sword bridge are found not to exist, or in which the tourney crowd consider Lancelot cowardly when he was merely obeying his lady's command. Thus, we are dealing with a work filled with consistently unreliable observers and narrators. Chrétien's method of filtering his story through others' eyes lends to it a further ambiguous cast which makes it impossible to assign ideas and positions to the author.

The purpose of all the techniques discussed here, from the presentation of an ambiguous hero to the systematic obscuring of narrative viewpoint, is still open to question, of course. It is tempting to identify Chrétien with his character, especially if we assume that each was required by obedience to his lady to perform acts which his code otherwise disapproved. But such an assumption in regard to the author may be unwarranted. Perhaps it is true that Chrétien disapproved of the task imposed on him; certainly he carried it out in such a way that the perceptive reader might reasonably question the soundness and wisdom of total obedience to the desires (or whims) of the courtly lady. Certainly he seems to have had considerable fun at the expense of his hero, of his genre, of the tradition he was treating. And certainly this fact and his particular use of narrative point of view offer ample evidence that he did not mindlessly endorse his theme or his hero. But I think they also prevent our simply identifying him with the opposite view. To suggest that Chrétien is in effect undermining his mission is, I think, to sell his art short, for he has accomplished something more remarkable—and difficult— than that. Unless we simply equate ambiguity with subversion, the continual shifting of Chrétien's viewpoint and his disappearance into the maze of his narrative stances simply obscure his intention; thus, he lends the weight of his narrative authority neither to the advocacy of *fin' amors* nor to its denunciation. The ambiguities of the work suggest that Chrétien left its meaning open; to the extent that the poem does reveal an author's attitude, it seems to be one of detached bemusement. In such a case, a particular reader may *choose* to read it as serious or as subversive, but unless a study of Chrétien's narrative procedures gives us reason to close the poem to one of these interpretations, we should leave it open.

Our natural impulse is perhaps to resolve ambiguities in favor of one position or the other. But to do so in the case of this romance would require our bringing it to a preconceived notion of what the author intended. The medieval mind and the medieval poem were apparently capable of accommodating ambiguities and disparities, and the simultaneous presentation of two contrasting views of the character and story provides much of the richness of this work. The irony of the poem should cause us to view it with the same degree of detachment with which Chrétien apparently conceived and executed it, and perhaps we should leave his ambiguities intact. He has written a very complex and sophisticated poem, and there is less persuasive evidence that he was attacking courtly love than that he was refusing to interpret for future readers and generations the meaning of his work.

Chrétien's primary characters are usually quite advanced when we first meet them. In most cases they are knights whose reputation is already made and known; Alexandre is prepared, when *Cligés* opens, to become a knight. In his final romance, Chrétien presents us a hero who is far from accomplished, and who, in fact, is apparently rather far even from being a hero in the usual sense of the word. If Gauvain consistently serves as the model of the cultured knight, most of the other knights are not far behind; they have a thorough command of their craft, they are (except for Alexandre) comfortable with the conventions of love and social intercourse—in short, they are properly sophisticated representatives of the social, political, and military phenomenon known as the Arthurian court. Perceval, however, is unlike any of them: his naiveté, his ingenuousness, his ignorance bring him closer to Candide than to anyone populating the Arthurian universe. If their psychological crisis causes the other characters to want to leave both their world and their consciousness behind them and begin, as I suggested, *tabula rasa*, they simply revert to a situation resembling Perceval's initial state. They start over; he must simply *start*. In fact, that is an overstatement, because they still retain their command of their martial art, which Perceval has never acquired—outside of hunting in the forest with *gavelos*. He is however eager to acquire those skills and any others that will make him a knight, for in ambition Arthur's court contains no one to compare with him. This character and his career fascinate readers and critics alike, and it may well be because, more than any other romance by Chrétien, this is the hero's own story. By that I do not mean simply that Chrétien focuses more sharply on him than on the heroes of his other works (although that may well be true), but that it is the story of Perceval's initial, exhilarating, and painful confrontation with the world. And specifically because it is the opaque consciousness of the naive hero which serves, more consistently than in the other romances, as the lens through which Chrétien's narrative passes in order to reach us.

Critics have generally assumed that Chrétien is systematically excluding us from knowledge of whatever Perceval does not know. The author is showing everything through Perceval's eyes in order to depict more effectively his awakening and his initiation. Thus, when the Grail procession passes before his eyes, it is described to us in all its splendor— but in all its mystery as well. It is *un graal*, in which Perceval sees nothing more than a marvelous object which excites his curiosity. What he does not know, we are not to know, and thus Chrétien offers no explanation of the Grail's significance. We will find out later what the Grail means— but only when his hero also discovers its significance.

In a general sense, this notion of Chrétien's technique has much to commend it. Dante's ignorant pilgrim provides a striking example of such exposition, and we have seen, even in Chrétien's first romance, that he will, when his art so dictates, deny us access to information not possessed by a particular character. In *Perceval* the hero's initiation into prowess, love, and society may be most effectively dramatized by showing us not simply what he *does* but what he sees and understands (or, more characteristically, fails to understand). Nonetheless, we need to define the poet's method with more precision. It is true that he usually filters his narrative through Perceval's eyes, but he does not always do so, for there are times when we do have knowledge denied to him. Indeed, Chrétien *must* make privileged observers of us if his comic and ironic view of his hero is to be effectively communicated, for that view depends on our knowing considerably more than the character does. Thus, if we had experienced through his consciousness the terrifying noises in his mother's forest, we would not find it at all strange that he thinks devils are approaching. His reaction may be naive, but it is comical only because Chrétien has told us that Perceval heard *five knights* approaching. Our knowledge is superior to his,[21] and that superiority enables us to laugh at the ignorant youth. Similarly, when he comes to the structure which matches his mother's description of a church, we expect more comedy— because Chrétien has told us it was a tent:

S'a a cheminer entendu
Tant que il vit un tref tendu
En une praerie bele
Les le rieu d'une fontenele.

(vss. 637-40)

In these episodes and numerous others, Chrétien tells us what we
need to know in order to understand his character, and in the process we
frequently receive knowledge Perceval does not have (including Chrétien's
direct reference to his hero's ignorance and opacity). With the two episodes
of Blancheflor and the Grail procession, Chrétien omits certain explanations which, judging by the critical confusion surrounding them, we do
need. These questions, concerning Perceval's possible dalliance with
Blancheflor and the meaning of the Grail, can be treated only with
reference to Chrétien's narrative method. That method has frequently
been considered in regard to the latter episode, rarely in relationship
to the former.

Opinion on the question of Perceval's and Blancheflor's sexual activities is thoroughly divided, from the notion that the substitution, in later
tradition, of Galahad for Perceval as the Grail hero gave evidence of the
latter's sinful past, to the quite categorical rejection by Holmes and Klenke
of the possibility that this youth destined for greatness would have indulged
such an appetite.[22] Peter Haidu's contention that nothing of a sexual nature
occurred between them is based in part on his study of structural and
thematic parallels between this episode and the previous one involving the
Tent Maiden (see pp. 156-58). In the earlier scene Perceval had assumed an
erotically suggestive position while, in obedience to the teaching of his
mother, contenting himself with a kiss. Considering the episodes to be dou-
lets, Haidu concludes that Perceval's virtue remained undefiled in the second as well. His suggestion is itself seductive, but not entirely convincing.
Throughout the work Perceval makes enormous progress—but in a
limited sense. He consistently demonstrates a precocious ability to learn
how to do what he has been told to do or what he considers will make him
into a knight. He has prodigious talent for the acquisition of chivalric
skills. And yet he acquires such skills without understanding their
meaning; similarly, he understands little or nothing of the world, and he
remains completely unaware of his own comical naiveté. If he is capable
of learning to use arms and armor without understanding them, it would
be entirely logical for his sexual initiation to occur in the same manner;
love-making, as well as warfare, can be reduced to a mechanical procedure,
and it is characteristic of Perceval to think solely in terms of procedure.
Thus, while he procured nothing more than a kiss from the Tent Maiden,

we might reasonably expect him to make additional progress in the acquisition of amorous skills without any essential advancement in his understanding or sense of responsibility.

Such an explanation seems to me the most satisfactory one in terms of what we know of Perceval's character and the early development of the story. Nonetheless, I have no doubt that it could be persuasively refuted, as can be Haidu's argument, as can be all the other arguments. The fact is that we do not know what happened between Perceval and Blancheflor that critical night simply because Chrétien does not tell us. They lay *bouche a boche, bras a bras* (vs. 2068), and unless we take that expression to be a euphemism (which it clearly is in some texts) for sexual intercourse, we have no concrete evidence to aid our analysis of the passage. And moreover, all discussions of the problem unfortunately obscure the most important elements of the episode, the motivation of the characters. *We* may be interested in knowing what happened after Perceval "l'a soz le covertoir mise" (vs. 2060), but there is no evidence that Chrétien was. Only two matters are finally significant here: the reason for her seducing him (sexually or no), and the reason for his agreeing to undertake her defense. On these two questions Chrétien is quite explicit:

Par tans se porra aloser
Li chevaliers, s'il faire l'ose,
C'onques cele por autre chose
Ne vint plorer desor sa face,
Que que ele entendant li face,
Fors por che qu'ele li meïst
En corage qu'il empreïst
La bataille, s'il l'ose emprendre
Por li, por sa terre desfendre.

(vss. 2038-46)

Here Perceval's motivation is entirely in character; it is enough for someone to suggest to him that "this is what knights do" or that "this is a way to win fame," and he will undertake such an action immediately. Blancheflor may have added sexual inducements, but if so they were superfluous diversions which Chrétien did not even find it necessary to describe. In fact, even her tears may have been superfluous: Perceval needs no persuading when he has a chance to play at chivalry. At this point, they are well matched to each other in selfishness, never hesitating to use each other for selfish ends. She uses what are traditionally considered "feminine wiles" (psychology and tears, if not sex) to gain his protection; he uses her despair as an opportunity to practice his skills and win fame. Whether they sleep together in the bargain is without consequence, literal or figurative: it simply does not matter. And while that conclusion will not put an end to speculation, it should on the other hand permit us to concentrate our attention on the significant elements of the scene: Blancheflor's deviousness (why not simply *ask* him to champion her cause?) and Perceval's habit of perverting chivalry, by subordinating the human needs which should justify it to the details of the chivalric process itself.

The points I have made in regard to the Blancheflor episode apply in part to the Grail Castle scene as well. I would not contend that the question of the Grail's meaning is irrelevant (Chrétien will later explain quite clearly what it is and what it represents). But it is true that its meaning is less important in this scene than the fact that Perceval does not *know* what it means and that for the time being he makes no effort to dispel his ignorance. Of course, it is not the Grail which possesses restorative powers, but the *question* about the Grail and the lance. In fact, the Grail is not even the object of the question Perceval should ask; it is only an instrument, the meaning of which is at this point defined in terms of its function. It protects and preserves, and that function both justifies it and confers importance on it. The parallel with chivalry is inevitable here. The knight has the opportunity to render responsible service to others, to protect and defend them, and if he does not avail himself of such an opportunity (that is, if he fails to define his chivalric vocation in terms of service), he is without justifiable purpose.

This reference to chivalry and to Perceval's own situation is only a symbolic association, and we would hardly expect him to grasp the subtlety of its application. But, of course, he fails to grasp *anything* of significance in this episode. He is no less curious here than he was when he first encountered knights, but there is one great difference: he has now become a knight himself. He has absorbed, with more or less success, the rules and precepts offered him by Gornemanz, and he ignorantly permits his chivalric code to serve constantly as a device to censor his natural (i.e., uncourtly, unknightly) impulses. Interestingly, he does not fail or refuse to ask the proper question; he simply postpones it (as he refused to postpone his departure from his mother and from Blancheflor, and as he repeatedly postponed his return to his mother). The effect is the same in either case: his failure corresponds to the failure of the chivalric code if it is not at the service of an unselfish ideal.

Perceval's silence has its counterpart in Chrétien's, for as I have suggested, we are generally shown only what the hero experiences. Perceval does not know who is served with the Grail, and as a result we share his ignorance. But once again, it is not quite true that we see *only* through his eyes, for while we learn nothing of the Fisher King's father, we do learn something of the future in store for Perceval:

Si criem que il n'i ait damage,
Por che que j'ai oï retraire
Qu'ausi se puet on bien trop taire
Com trop parler a la foie[e].

(vss. 3248-51)

The suggestion that Chrétien filters his entire narrative through the consciousness of his main character is appealing, and such a technique would be entirely in harmony with methods the poet has used elsewhere. But I confess that I am not entirely satisfied with this explanation for certain aspects of Chrétien's last romance. First of all, as I have stressed, Chrétien offers us at every turn the information we need for an understanding of Perceval. Through much of the story his view of his hero is comic, and the comedy is strengthened by our possession of knowledge which he does not have. Chrétien permits us to see things with a clear, or only slightly jaundiced, eye, whereas Perceval misconstrues the smallest detail and the most momentous event alike. Moreover, the change in the Grail, from splendid and mysterious object to a holy relic (*tant sainte chose est li graals*: vs. 6425) strikes me as too violent a transformation to be explained simply as a reflection of Perceval's gradual awakening. Finally, it is a somewhat disturbing development, not common to Chrétien's art, to find emphasis transferred from an object's function to the object itself, but this is what happens in the hermit episode. In the earlier scene, as I have noted, the Grail is important because someone is served with it (a fact that determines the form and substance of the Grail question), and it is important as the impetus for the question—which however remains unasked. The Grail itself is a marvelous object, of course, but it is its function (its thematic function in sustaining the old king, its narrative function in providing an opportunity for the question) which gives it significance. Yet, later, in a passage fairly drenched in mystic and religious rhetoric, we learn that it is itself a *tant sainte chose*. Chrétien normally has his characters embrace objects as ends in themselves and only later grasp their meaning and use; that he would in this case move from an emphasis on the Grail's function to an insistence on its own character and its rigid symbolic association is not inconceivable, but in my opinion it does a disservice to his art,[23] and it is in any case a phenomenon which must remain an enigma, because Chrétien was unable to complete his masterpiece.

In all his works, nonetheless, and in practically all their detail, Chrétien shows himself a sensitive master of narrative method, intruding where necessary, keeping his silence where needed, moving from one "center of consciousness" to another when it will serve his purposes, intuitively altering his technique to generate the necessary literary response. *Perceval*, his last work, presents problems in this respect, but only in the final scene of the hero's adventures. Otherwise, Chrétien's technical procedures permit him to combine in that work an effective depiction of the comical and candid youth (who appears however to have greatness in store for him), a penetrating social critique, and an intriguingly mysterious and mystical drama. In any consideration of the fascination this work has held for readers, we must take into account the interest of Chrétien's *matière* (and in particular the archetypical appeal of the Grail itself), and we cannot discount the historical accident which left the work uncompleted and many questions unresolved. But be that as it may, Chrétien's pride in the prologue of *Erec* was not misplaced, for in all his works the narrative matter, from whatever source and of whatever intrinsic appeal, simply provided the grist for the mill of his fictional artistry. His narrative techniques, his uses of perspective and point of view, provide one important element in his process of *conjointure*; the other major element is, as we shall see, form—the physical and thematic construction of the poems themselves.

CHAPTER IV

FORM

The critic approaching Chrétien's works with a view to the analysis of form sets himself a formidable task, simply because of their multiplicity of structures. There are few, perhaps no, formal procedures characteristic of twelfth-century literature which are not also used by Chrétien. Of course, he is both receiver and originator of such procedures: some of them, traditional in nature, he found ideal for his purposes; in other cases writers certainly borrowed methods, as well as themes and motifs, from him. Bi- or tripartition, centrality and symmetrical composition, structural tensions created by juxtaposition, repetition (and repetition with inversion or variation)—all are common features of the physical structure of Chrétien's romances. Most of these features are easily identified in any of his works and will require little explanation outside of the references I will make to them in my analysis of an individual poem. It may however be useful to preface those analyses by a brief discussion of interlace and analogy, the two most significant form-conferring principles developed by the poet.

Interlace, or *entrelacement*, is as familiar a principle to medievalists as are the others I mentioned above, but it may be most familiar in a thirteenth-century context, in its use as an organizing technique in the *Prose Lancelot*. Ferdinand Lot,[1] who provided the basic study of that work and who therein applied the term *entrelacement* to its organizational system, traced a large number of themes and episodes which the poet would introduce, drop, and resume many pages later, perhaps several times. These themes are thus "interlaced" one with another, and the resumption serves to tie together sections of the poem that are related to each other but not necessarily to those which immediately precede or follow them. The effect, as described by Vinaver,[2] is like that of a tapestry: ". . . a single cut across it, made at any point, would unravel it all." The result is a loosely-knit but thoroughly composed structure. All the threads will eventually be tied up, and all the themes taken to their completion, but the links between consecutive episodes are often vague or virtually non-existent. Interlace was thus an important tool of the poet dealing with complex or multiple narratives. It required the audience to keep in their minds a large amount of information and a large number of characters and plots, but because the resumption of a theme is always implied by its introduction and abandonment, interlace simplified the author's task of maintaining audience interest. The listener was led at every turn to anticipate the return of a number of themes and subjects. The use of interlace suggests that both the idea of a single, uncomplicated plot line and that of separable chapters of a story were foreign to the esthetics of the romance. An additional possibility for the author who composes by juxtaposing blocks of material related to different themes or characters is the creation of irony and contrast; even small differences between consecutive but unrelated episodes can portray larger differences between the psychology or the morality of two characters.

Chrétien uses interlace extensively in the construction of his romances, but it is a kind of interlace which requires some word of explanation here. It is generally not applied to multiple quests and stories in Chrétien, except in the case of Gauvain; there, particularly in the later works, we find Gauvain's adventures either juxtaposed to or partially interlaced with those of the hero. More frequently, Chrétien uses interlace as a way of organizing the adventures of a single character into a coherent and esthetically satisfying sequence; thus in *Perceval* we find almost rhythmically inserted references to the hero's postponed avenging of the smiling maiden, an *intended* quest which is interlaced with his other quests (he finally does avenge her, quite by accident, in his battle with Keu). It is however in *Yvain* that Chrétien will combine to best esthetic advantage the simple idea of an interrupted event with the symmetrical organization of episodes.

The term "analogy" will immediately call to mind the chapter "Analogy as the Dominant Form" in Vinaver's *The Rise of Romance*, where the technique receives quite thorough treatment. The nature of literary analogy is quite simple: it consists of two or more episodes which resemble each other or, more subtly, contain certain *elements* which resemble each other. Of the function of analogy, Vinaver states (*Rise of Romance*, p. 105): ". . . the juxtaposition of analogous incidents can be used as a means of bringing to light something which would otherwise have remained unknown or unexplained. The result is a widening of the forms of 'understanding' . . . ." This reference to "understanding" must recall to us the contention of Aquinas that it is through analogy that we may comprehend truth,[3] and it is similarly through analogy that we are shown relationships between episodes or events of a narrative, relationships which may exist independent of causal or temporal links and which may even be more strongly established because of this causal independence. In many works, analogical composition refers not simply to resemblances between episodes, but specifically to the fashioning of episodes so that their resemblances relate them all to the major theme of the work. In other words, it is a method of composing by which a major theme or episode, constituting a nucleus, is reflected in a variety of other episodes which share with it certain narrative elements or images. In its most general sense, what I have called Chrétien's use of the *contrappasso* provides an illustration of analogy, since the expiation is related in kind to the offense. Thus, in *Erec et Enide*, the motifs of silence and broken silence established in the crisis scene are repeatedly reflected in those of the imposed and broken silence of the quest sequence. Throughout the poem, a number of miscellaneous episodes incorporate some motif, or contain some reflection, of the central intrigue of the work.

This example illustrates the nature of analogy, but the example is less than apt because analogy here reinforces causality (the expiation resembles the offense because it is caused by it), whereas analogical methods frequently link events without apparent connection. Thus, analogy need not function merely as a method of elucidation of an event; its justification may frequently be more esthetic than thematic or explicative; the structure of the work comprises any perceptible system of organization which "holds it together," which confers a degree of cohesiveness on it, and in Chrétien's poems it is the analogical relationship of one episode to many others which associates them in our minds. Of course, the recognition of analogy does not simply eliminate the notion of causality, but it modifies it profoundly. Events are not necessarily *caused* in the direct way we normally use the term, but those which share some motif or element, which are somehow alike in form or function, must be felt to be related in more than a casual way. In a sense, the kind of relationship established by analogy is more complex than our notion of causality, just as medieval symbolism is ultimately more complex than its modern equivalent. And certainly it is more than simple resemblance, which could be taken as an indication of a poet's poverty of imagination. Analogy appears in fact to be related to symbolism in that both functioned through a third term. In symbolism that term is an essential attribute shared by the other two; in an example proposed by Huizinga, white roses and virgins are related not because of any passing resemblance but because the beauty and tenderness they share are realities, and not just names for accidental and physically observable traits.[4] In regard to analogy, we are sometimes dealing with episodes which are simple doublets,[5] but more often they develop dissimilar narrative contours while sharing a term, a motif or image, or, quite often, a structure. And just as symbolism expresses, in Huizinga's words, "a mysterious connection between two ideas" (p. 186), analogy in literary composition apparently provided a mysterious expression of relationships between events and actions. Resemblance serves as evidence for relationship (although the mystery of the connection would itself seem to be essential: things are "somehow" related), and I have suggested elsewhere that this relationship provides a coherent—as well as cohesive—form for the work.[6]

One further aspect of analogy should be noted here. In its most basic and apparent function, analogy is a principle permitting the horizontal amplification or dilation of the work by the addition of episodes, themes, and characters which reflect the main motifs of the poem. It should be noted, however, that analogy is not simply a device for the linear multiplication of episodes: it is also a vertical phenomenon, operating on various levels of meaning. That is, the choice of narrative detail reflects, and appears to be determined in part by, the ethical concerns and the psychology and motivation of the characters. Thus, even though episodes can be spun out at great length, they are carefully integrated into a fully unified work. Moreover, this technique profoundly affects the character of the romance in another way, for events and narrative developments with no logical connection with a character's intent nonetheless seem to be somehow psychologically determined. In other words, the same facts and forces which determine a character's reaction to events also appear to determine those events themselves and create an impression of inevitability (cf. Vinaver, *Rise of Romance*, p. 106).

A convenient example of this vertical expansion by analogy is provided by *Erec et Enide*. When at the beginning of the work Erec, unarmed, remains behind with the queen while all the other knights precede them, no explanation for his action is given—or needed. Yet, it will become clear later that this episode, with no implication of cowardice or sloth on Erec's part, simply foreshadows the exposition of his recreance with Enide. The original episode is nonfunctional on the level of motivation, but its narrative elements are clearly shaped by the central ethical and psychological situation of the work.

The same principle is at work in *Cligés*. It is generally agreed that the central problem of this poem is the characters' reaction to love: Alexandre's concealment of it and resistance to it, as opposed to Cligés's acceptance of it as a natural and desirable emotion. But once the motifs of concealment and revelation are established in this psychological context, they move immediately to inform all parts of the poem, not only on the level of motivation, as in my first example from *Erec*, but also on the level of story itself. Thus, we have a proliferation of episodes involving, for example, disguised soldiers or concealed armies who are revealed by the sudden light of the moon. Such episodes rarely exhibit any logical link with the character's motivation; they simply utilize, on another level, some motif or some pattern of imagery or diction which was previously developed in relation to the ethical or psychological dimension of the story.

Thus when love is concealed, we may expect also the narrative concealment of identities, armies, etc.

One additional example, from the *Chevalier de la Charrette*: the significance of the cart is clear enough, but we might also note that, in the physical (i.e., spatial) constitution of the narrative, it is simply one member of an elaborate system of confining or containing objects, ranging from beds to rooms to towers to prisons. The central symbol of the work, with its implications for the character of Lancelot, determines the nature of the poem's imagistic system: and while most of the other images have a narrative function, they lack the cart's relationship to its occupant.

Thus, to a considerable extent, analogy functions not only to expand the work horizontally but also to relate character and theme to the smallest details of the narrative. Once any theme is established, it tends to generate its own analogues; and just as one episode of the work may be related to another by a common form or theme, so are objects related to ideas and, in turn, to the poet's moral concerns. The result is a web of connections, extending both horizontally and vertically throughout the poem, foreshadowing and echoing each other. The absence of logical links between many scenes and motifs gives to the work the effect of gratuitousness characteristic of the hero's adventures, but at the same time analogical composition gives the impression of carefully controlled cohesiveness within a thoroughly organized fictional universe. As a result, Chrétien's works attain a definite unity (but a unity totally unlike that of later literature) without sacrificing the variety of detail which has never failed to fascinate his audiences.

In the pages that follow, I deal for the most part with the spatial (or architectural) and thematic construction of Chrétien's poems, their "shape," but as my discussion of analogy suggests, the inseparability of form and meaning imposes itself in his works with the same force as the axiomatic inseparability of form and content in all literature. Indeed, as I have suggested, form *is* meaning, or at least a good part of it, for Chrétien; for the structure and sequence of the hero's adventures, the relationship of expiation to offense, the patterns which, once established in the works, imply a completion and point toward the form and method of its accomplishment, and especially the "vertical" connections between motivation and event and between character and imagery—all these structural features of Chrétien's poems give valid and effective expression to the problems treated therein and to the meaning which emerges. It may be true that in the act of composition (*conjointure*), the poet derives a meaning (a *sens*) from his material, but the narrative act itself retains great importance for Chrétien, and because his material was for the most part quite traditional, it was by technique that he distinguished himself from the mass of story-tellers.

Erec et Enide

Despite the persistence of disputes regarding the number of sections or divisions contained within *Erec et Enide* (and within the other romances as well),[7] the basic tripartition of its physical structure is quite clear. Critics who arrive at numbers other than three are generally basing their count, with thorough justification but from a different point of view, on the thematic division of the poem, or on the division into sections dealing with love and society, or perhaps on the stages of the hero's progress, but not on an analysis of physical structure. It is with the last that I wish to begin, although my earlier remarks have already suggested the possibility of a thematic duality based on the hero's descent and ascent; that is, on his state before and after the crisis.

In Chrétien's first romance, more than any other, the division between sections is strongly marked; indeed, the poet marks it explicitly between the first and second parts, with the statement *Ici fenist li premiers vers* (vs. 1796).[8] Chrétien does not refer so directly to the end of the second *vers* and the beginning of the last, but that division is nonetheless apparent. At vs. 5318, the dramas have been resolved, the offenses expiated, the lessons learned, and the lovers reconciled; there is, in other words, every reason for the story to end here—except that Chrétien's treatment of a theme requires not only development and demonstration, but confirmation as well. Thus we follow Erec through the adventure known as the "Joie de la Cort," the main component of the final division.

If we examine these divisions further, we encounter a minor difficulty in the fact that the reconciliation of Erec and Enide does not immediately precede the Joie de la Cort episode. There is an intervening episode. At the apparent end of their wandering, Erec informs her:

. . . . "Ma dolce suer,
Bien vos ai de tot essaiee.
Or ne soiez plus esmaiee,
C'or vos aim plus qu'ainz mes ne fis,
Et je resui certains et fis
Que vos m'amez parfitemant.
Or voel estre d'or en avant,
Ausi con j'estoie devant,
Tot a vostre comandemant;
Et se vos rien m'avez mesdit,

Je le vos pardoing tot et quit
Del forfet et de la parole."

                    (vss. 4882-93)

And then Chrétien adds a lyrically effective closure to the scene:

Adons la rebeise et acole.
Or n'est pas Enyde a maleise,
Quand ses sires l'acole et beise,
Et de s'amor la raseüre.
Par nuit s'an vont grant aleüre,
Et ce lor fet grant soatume
Que la nuit luisoit cler la lune.

                    (vss. 4894-4900)

In the scene which then separates this one from the Joie de la Cort, Erec, wounded and weak, is attacked for the second time by Guivret le Petit. The hero falls from his horse and is saved by the intervention of his wife. Recognizing the two of them, Guivret has Erec cared for, and the three of them set out together for Arthur's court. Only then does Erec learn of the marvelous adventure of the Joie de la Cort and resolve to seek it.

If we consider the reconciliation of the knight and his lady as the conclusion of the central section—and I think we must take it as a thematic climax at very least—there emerges from the narrative a remarkable example of symmetrical structure. The poem divides quite naturally into three parts, concluded respectively by Erec's and Enide's marriage, their reconciliation, and their coronation—three natural and effective conclusions to the diverse sequences of the work. These three events depict the lovers' union, then their re-union, and finally the confirmation of their union and of their worth and position. Preceding these three climaxes we find three other episodes (or complexes of episodes) which correspond roughly to one another by their function and meaning. In the first section it is the battle for the sparrow-hawk, which constitutes a demonstration of Erec's valor and which, more significantly, represents the winning of Enide. Preceding their reconciliation in the middle division is the full quest (itself a sequence of episodes which however function as a single element in Chrétien's narrative development),[9] in which Erec again— and repeatedly—gives proof of his valor and which depicts the re-winning of Enide. The Joie de la Cort scene confirms not only his prowess but her proper role as well, and at the same time, Erec liberates another knight from the same kind of activity which had brought about his own crisis.

There remains the initial scene in each structural triad. The essential one of these is the second, the scene of Erec's recreance and Enide's speech.

In the analysis of the remaining three episodes, we must have reference to the earlier discussion of analogy, for the first scene (the hunt for the white stag) and the third (Erec's second encounter with Guivret) present analogical correspondences with the important recreance scene. When, at the beginning of the story, Arthur orders the hunt for the white stag, all the knights set out fully armed. Erec, the exception to this statement, has not adequately armed himself, and he leaves the group to ride behind with the queen: "Je ne ving ça por autre afere/Fors por vos conpaignie fere" (vss. 109-10). The incident is noteworthy, since we would reasonably expect him to be competing with the other knights and displaying his valor in the hunt. Without condemning Erec's actions, Chrétien has simply given us the first example of a knight who chooses to remain with a lady rather than to seek adventure. In recounting this occurrence in the first division of the story, Chrétien is foreshadowing the central situation with Erec and Enide, but in the Guivret episode he echoes a different aspect of the same situation. This time Erec's inactivity is not the result of negligence or distraction from his duty; it is due simply to his physical state. He is easily defeated by his opponent, and as he lies on the ground, lacking the strength to rise, it is Enide who rushes forward to defend him, praising him, explaining his condition, and pleading for mercy. This episode is but one of a number in which she breaks her silence to warn or save her husband, but both Erec's position (lying prone near her) and her verbal intervention relate this scene specifically to the crisis episode. There is no suggestion that Erec is still guilty of recreance or that he is in any way responsible for his pitiful state in this scene; the episode contains no new implications for character or motivation. Yet, its location and its narrative development recall the earlier episode and establish an analogical—but not *logical*—connection between them. Notably, this scene serves another purpose as well; with Erec rendered inactive here, she becomes active in her concern for him; the episode provides a confirmation of her essentially correct, responsible, and unselfish behavior. It is a vindication of her earlier concern for Erec's reputation, if not of the pride which caused her to utter the tragic words. This episode is followed by the confirmation of *Erec's* character and situation, for in the Joie de la Cort scene Enide is left behind while he actively pursues adventure and fame, as he rightly should.

The structural configuration of the poem, as I have traced it here, can be summarized conveniently as follows:

I.
{
1. Hunt: a prefiguration of recreance
2. Sparrow Hawk: the winning of Enide
3. Wedding: the union of Erec and Enide
}

II. $\begin{cases} \text{1. Crisis: Erec's recreance} \\ \text{2. Quest: the re-winning of Enide} \\ \text{3. Reconciliation: the reunion of Erec and Enide} \end{cases}$

III. $\begin{cases} \text{1. Guivret: an echo of recreance (and Enide's vindication)} \\ \text{2. Joy of the Court: confirmation of Erec's valor (and an} \\ \text{\quad analogy of his and Enide's situation)} \\ \text{3. Coronation: reunion and ascension} \end{cases}$

I have of course left until now the problem of the multiplicity of episodes comprising the quest, because, as I indicated, they *function* as a single step in the poem's narrative and thematic development. However, these scenes add an additional argument for the tripartition of the work, for the quest is itself composed of three parts, each of which consists of one or two adventures, followed by a stay (however reluctant) in a castle or in Arthur's camp.[10] First, Erec is attacked by three and then by five knights; after dispatching his adversaries, he and Enide spend the night in the forest and then accept an invitation to a castle in the vicinity (I discuss the castle scenes later). The following day, he does battle with Guivret and later with Keu; after some coaxing by Gauvain, he and Enide agree to stay the night in the camp of Arthur and Guenevere. In the third sequence, he rescues Cadoc by killing two giants, but then, weakened, he collapses and is taken to another castle. We might reasonably allow ourselves to be guided by the principle of centrality in these sequences (as we legitimately were in the general structure of the work), and the brief but important contact Erec establishes with the Arthurian court in the very middle of the quest would argue for such an approach. However, we should see in Erec's and Enide's adventures a progression which violates, or at least overrides, their centrality. In the first series of adventures (culminating in the first castle scene) Erec responds to nothing but threats and attacks directed at him from without; otherwise, he maintains his petulant silence and appears devoid of any normal human reactions. In the second group, he is still responding to similar attacks, but he has softened his attitude toward Enide and moderated his treatment of her; and toward the end of this section he shows himself capable of conducting a normal and quite civil conversation with Gauvain. In the third section, for the first time, he voluntarily undertakes action for a reason other than the testing of himself and Enide (to rescue Cadoc); he has now progressed to the point of using prowess and adventure for their intended purpose. This fact signals an important change in his attitude toward his wife, and it indicates that the quest is nearing its end.

The structural elements which I have thus far defined serve as important building materials for Chrétien, and their arrangement into groups and symmetrical patterns proves esthetically satisfying (tripartition, of course, is intrinsically satisfying, and it is a method Chrétien uses often). Furthermore, the analogical relationships established between certain episodes, which function in similar ways or which utilize similar motifs, give a further cohesiveness to the work's form. Yet, analogy is a far more significant feature of that form than my remarks have thus far indicated. Composition for the medieval poet implied the literary amplification of a theme or an idea,[11] and Chrétien effects this amplification in *Erec* by incorporating into the narrative a number of episodes which may have only a general relation to the central situation or theme, but which are in fact prefigurations or recollections of it. Thus, while these incidents advance the narrative, they also reflect or restate the theme of the work and serve as an organizing force in the romance.

I· have noted that Erec reacts against his recreance by excessive activity and against Enide's presumption in speaking by a command that she remain silent. Immediately after that command and their departure, Erec finds himself in a series of perilous situations, attacked by three knights, then by five, later by Count Galoain with one hundred men, and finally by a single knight, Guivret. Each time, Enide thinks he is unaware of the danger. That she breaks her silence on these occasions as well is not unexpected, but it is significant. She was previously faced with the choice of incurring Erec's wrath if she spoke out, or seeing him lose his reputation if she did not. Now she has a similar choice: if she warns him of the danger, she may lose his love, but otherwise he may lose his life. In every case, she speaks and Erec rebukes her, but his reproaches become progressively less severe, until she is at last forgiven. Realizing that love and concern are the reasons for her present disobedience, Erec evidently concludes that her motives were the same when she first offended him. This broken silence, which convinces Erec of her love, corresponds to the broken silence which made him doubt that love; it is by repeating her act that she begins to justify it.[12]

The wanderings of Erec and Enide include two other incidents which reflect aspects of the main intrigue. Yet the similarities might be considered a mere coincidence, were it not for the obvious significance that Chrétien attaches to the episodes, for they mark the two principal stages in Enide's expiation. Moreover, the two adventures are notable in that they both concern counts who have fallen in love with Enide.

The first of these episodes, just prior to the attack by the hundred knights, involves Count Galoain, who resolves to kill Erec and marry his

wife. The deception that Enide practices on him to save Erec is itself a
mock love test, and an examination of the episode will demonstrate that
it is intended as a parallel to the real love test to which Erec subjects her.
Although brief, it appears in fact to be an incident of prime importance
for the development of the work.

When Enide offends Erec by speaking of his recreance, she admits
her guilt and acknowledges that she was acting out of pride (vss. 2602-
03; 3110-12). This pride is expressed not by her listening to or repeating
the rumors (for her concern is understandable), but by her fear that *she*
would be blamed for the apparent change in Erec:

"Molt me poise quant an l'an dit
Et por ce m'an poise ancor plus
Qu'il m'an metent le blasme sus;
Blasmee an sui, ce poise moi."

(vss. 2554-57)

Thus, at the heart of Enide's offense is not only a possible doubt of Erec's
prowess but also an explicit concern for her own reputation.

The mock love test occurs almost exactly in the middle of their quest.
Count Galoain, visiting them at night, speaks with Enide and remarks
that Erec obviously no longer cares for her. He solicits her love and
promises her better treatment. Without hesitation, Enide refuses his
attentions, and he accuses her of speaking hastily, out of pride (vss. 3347-
50). It is notable that in the episode of the mock love text he accuses her
of the very sin which, by her own admission, she had earlier committed.
The count now threatens to kill Erec, and to save him Enide pleads a
concern for her own reputation, the same concern which had been the
partial cause of her problems in the first place:

"Trop grant mesprison ferïez,
Et g'en reseroie blasmee:
Tuit diroient par la contree
Que ce seroit fet par mon los."

(vss. 3368-71)

She assures the count that she was only testing his love and that she will
be his if he will postpone his actions until the following morning. Her
deception is successful, and she is able to warn Erec, thereby saving his
life while remaining faithful to him.

It seems clear that the parallel between the true and the mock love
tests is not coincidental. While her love is being cruelly tested by Erec,
she in her wisdom uses the analogue of this trial as a way of saving him and
proving herself to him. There is a further irony in the parallel of Enide's
emotions and motives in the two incidents. Her pride and concern for her

reputation, which cause her husband to question her love, are the very excuse which she now offers in order to save his life. Striking as these similarities are in themselves, they are made more significant by the fact that Chrétien clearly intended the incident as a turning point in the story. When Enide awakens Erec and explains her stratagem to him, we are told that he now learns how loyal she is (vss. 3480-81). Although their trials are far from over, this is the first indication that Erec is becoming convinced of her love. Consequently, his next admonition to her, as the count and his hundred knights pursue them, is tempered by an important reservation: she will pay dearly for her speech, *unless he changes his mind* (vs. 3560).

Thus Chrétien, composing an episode of central importance for his *roman*, has underlined that importance by making of the adventure an analogue of his main intrigue. Not only its narrative outline, but also Enide's motives and diction, reflect her dilemma just as she is working out a solution for it.

The next pivotal incident in the quest concerns the second count,[13] Oringle de Limors, and relates Enide's final success in proving her love. Here, Chrétien links the episode both to the scene in which Erec comes to doubt her love and to the scene of the first count, when she begins to prove herself. After rescuing Cadoc de Tabriol, Erec collapses from his wounds, and Enide thinks he is dead. The count arrives and takes Erec's body to his castle, after which he marries Enide against her will. That evening, she quarrels bitterly with the count; he strikes her and she responds:

"Ahi! fet ele, ne me chaut
Que tu me dies ne ne faces:
ne criem tes cos ne tes menaces.
Asez me bat, asez me fier:
Ja tant ne te troverai fier
Que por toi face plus ne mains,
Se tu or androit a tes mains
Me devoies les ialz sachier
Ou tote vive detranchier."
(vss. 4806-14)

As Enide is uttering these words, Erec recovers consciousness "ausi come hom qui s'esvoille" (vs. 4817). This statement—that he is like a man awaking from sleep—seems unnecessary in the context; yet, it does recall to us the earlier scene in which he did awake from sleep. In that instance, he roused himself to hear Enide speak of his recreance and to force her then to embark with him on their quest. Now, at the conclusion of their trials, Erec again awakes to hear Enide's voice. Moreover, like the previous scene involving a count, this episode was obviously of great significance

for Chrétien. Twice Erec awakens to hear Enide speaking; in one case her
words make him doubt her love and in the other they remove any
remaining doubt:

> C'or vos aim plus qu'ainz mes ne fis,
> Et je resui certains et fis
> Que vos m'amez parfitement.

(vss. 4885-87)

Clearly, Chrétien intends the castle scene to recall the bedroom scene
between Erec and Enide. The structural significance of this recollection is
obvious: Erec's awakening introduces the lengthy love test, into the middle
of which is inserted the mock love test, and which concludes with Erec's
second awakening. Moreover, these scenes mark the principal stages in
Enide's trial: Erec doubts her, he begins to believe that she loves him, and
his doubt is completely removed. Finally, these last two stages are linked
together, as I have stated, because they both concern counts who love
Enide. One wants to kill Erec, the other thinks he is already dead, and they
both offer Enide better treatment than she has been receiving at the hands
of her husband.

Now Erec and Enide are reconciled, but Erec has yet to seek the
adventure known as the Joie de la Cort. In a garden he finds a row of stakes
on which there are human heads, and one stake from which a horn is
suspended. Further on, he sees a lady seated on a couch. A knight
challenges him, and Erec wins the ensuing battle. The defeated knight,
Mabonagrain, explains the Joie de la Cort to him. The lady on the couch,
who is his mistress, had extracted a promise from him without telling
him what it was. Having made the promise, he is obliged by her to remain
in the garden until some other knight defeats him. Mabonagrain says that
her intention was to keep him shut up with her for the rest of his life
(vss. 6040-41). Meanwhile, Enide speaks with the lady, and it is revealed
that the two are cousins.

It is at this point that the technique which I am discussing is put to
best use. This final episode is first of all a further illustration of Erec's valor,
but it also presents a specific reflection of his and Enide's earlier flaws.
As Erec had abandoned chivalric endeavor to devote himself to amorous
pleasures, so has Mabonagrain long remained with his lady instead of
leaving to try his valor or win the reputation he deserves. The difference
between the two knights is that, as Mabonagrain points out, he is blame-
less, since he was only keeping a promise he had made. Similarly, Erec
had seen his own reputation suffer because he had ceased to frequent
tourneys; however, his recreance had been his own choice, for he had given
up adventure to remain with Enide. The most striking contrast is between

the ladies; the mistress of Mabonagrain has forced him to remain with her, while Enide was distressed because Erec neglected his duties for her sake. Chrétien makes use of such details as the women's tears to make the contrast more explicit; whereas Enide wept because Erec no longer went to tourneys, her cousin now weeps because Mabonagrain will henceforth be free to do so.

Thus, Mabonagrain and Enide's cousin are in a sense the counterparts of Erec and Enide. Chrétien uses the episode and the ladies' roles to emphasize differences between the couples, to recall the central intrigue and theme of the work, and to underscore Enide's innocence and virtue.

Each episode of this romance has a definite function in the poem and a clear relation to the incidents which precede and follow it, and in most cases this relation is analogically determined. Enide could certainly have proved her constancy, and Erec his prowess, without his command that she remain silent during the quest, and without the scenes of the counts who love Enide. Yet the poet's use of the incidents as a method of recapitulation gives to the work a thematic unity which replaces the logical unity sometimes lacking in episodic romances. Chrétien exploits the same technique in the scenes of the hunt and the Joie de la Cort, although these adventures recall not just a single element of the intrigue, but the entire theme of Erec's recreance.

In addition, it should be noted that Chrétien's method of amplification frequently works by contrast. Enide's speech proves her love and thus justifies her earlier speech which made Erec doubt her. A false love test reflects a true one. Erec awakes to be convinced of Enide's love, as he awoke to doubt it. Finally, the knight forced to give up chivalry stands in contrast to the one who had erred in doing so voluntarily.

Although I have examined some of the major episodes of the romance, the technique which I have discussed also accounts in many cases for Chrétien's choice of details. For example, Erec brings Enide to court dressed in rags, contrasting vividly with the beauty of her face and character. The next time they travel together is during the quest, when Erec emphasizes her guilt and presumption by contrasting them to the rich dress which he has forced her to wear.

In conclusion, even though *Erec* is the first of Chrétien's Arthurian romances, we find in it not only his talent for story-telling, but the attention to form and detail which will make of him the greatest practitioner of the genre. The perceptible patterns and the multiple links analogy establishes among episodes combine to confer on the work a remarkable clarity of form without detracting from the narrative expansiveness and variety which are the life-blood of romance.

Cligés

With the possible exception of *Perceval*, and for entirely different reasons, *Cligés* is Chrétien de Troyes's most perplexing romance. The author repeatedly interrupts the narrative to permit the characters to speak long monologues which, despite their effectiveness in the depiction of emotional states and the creation of distance and irony, many readers find distracting. Furthermore, the action shifts from Greece to Britain and back again, with occasional scenes set in Brittany and Germany. The very interpretation of the work presents problems: is it in fact an "anti-Tristan," as it is frequently considered, or a "neo-Tristan," or a "proto-Tristan," or, perhaps, a "super-Tristan"? An additional difficulty concerns form: sharply divided into two parts whose relationship has not always been clearly understood, the work proceeds rather haphazardly, its more or less chronological development fragmented by the numerous monologues on love and generosity. It is this matter of form or structure with which these pages will deal, although in *Cligés* no less than the other romances, many other problems—of theme, meaning, etc.—are inextricably bound up with this one.

The most conspicuous structural feature of *Cligés* is the bipartite division to which I have already referred: after stating his intention to tell the story of Cligés, Chrétien postpones it for some 2400 lines in order to recount first the adventures of Alexandre and Soredamors. It has been suggested that Chrétien is simply following his model (the Tristan story) in speaking of the father's life before that of the son and hero. Given Chrétien's usual attention to balance and unity, this answer must strike us as accurate but inadequate; rather, an examination will reveal that the two parts are related not only chronologically but also thematically and structurally.

In the first half of the work, Chrétien traces the effects of repressed love on Alexandre and Soredamors, who, despite their nobility, are strangers to this emotion. During the boat trip across the channel, they are smitten by love but refuse to admit it, not only to one another, but for a time to themselves as well. It is their refusal to recognize and admit their love which causes all their anguish:

Adés croist l'amors et si monte;
Mes li uns a de l'autre honte,
Si se cuevre et çoile chascuns,
Si que n'an pert flame ne funs
Del charbon qui est soz la cendre.
Por ce n'est pas la chalors mandre,

Einçois dure la chalors plus
Desoz la cendre que desus.

(vss. 593-600)

Their repressed love inspires Alexandre's monologues on his distress, the eyes, and love's arrow, and then Soredamors's discourse on her name and on love. Later, Soredamors wants to speak to Alexandre but does not know how to address him, and the two find frequent excuses to sit near each other, never having the courage to speak of the subject that torments them. It is finally the queen who tells them (vss. 2241 ff.) that she knows they are in love. She counsels them to admit rather than to conceal their love, telling them:

"Or vos lo que ja ne querez
Force ne volanté d'amor.
Par mariage et par enor
Vos antre aconpaigniez ansanble."

(vss. 2264-67)

Thus, the theme of the first portion of the work is the repression of love and the effects of that repression. The idea of conccalment, developed in the story of Alexandre and Soredamors, also provides the thematic link between the first and second parts. When Cligés and Fénice see each other for the first time, we are told that they fell in love: Cligés is *par amors conduit* (vs. 2760), and she, "Par boene amor, non par losange, / Ses ialz li baille et prant les suens" (vss. 2768-69). Fénice describes her joy and her distress to Thessala and soon speaks with Cligés of their feelings. Thus, whereas Alexandre and Soredamors concealed their love, Cligés and Fénice have no desire to hide theirs. The obstacles in the way of *their* love are purely external. The problem facing them is not that they refuse to admit their love to themselves and to each other, but that, owing to her marriage to Alis, they cannot reveal it to others. Alexandre and Soredamors resisted love and then concealed it through fear, while Cligés and Fénice, who would welcome love, have concealment forced upon them by circumstances. Thus, the basic structural principle of the work is the opposition of concealment and revelation.

In his elaboration of these themes, Chétien uses to excellent advantage the juxtaposition of events from his two generations of characters. As Peter Haidu has remarked, practically every episode in the first half of the poem has a close parallel in the second (p. 98). For example, the advice given to Alexandre before his journey to Arthur's court corresponds structurally to that which he later gives to Cligés, and the father's departure parallels the son's departure for Germany. Both trips are followed by the characters' discovery of love, and that by their first chivalric experiences

(Alexandre's knighting, Cligés's first battle). The structural relationships continue with scenes depicting the lovesickness of the two men, and here Chrétien introduces the symbol of each love. For Alexandre and Soredamors it is the golden hair which she has sewn into his shirt and which will periodically provoke his flights of ecstasy. The hair serves not only as a symbol and reminder of Alexandre's and Soredamors's love but as the actual instrument by which it was discovered and encouraged by the queen. For Cligés and Fénice the symbol is of course the potion. Thessala, whose function corresponds generally to that of Guenevere in the first half of the story and specifically to Brangien's in the Tristan story, prepares the wondrous potion which will give Alis the illusion that he is enjoying the favors of his wife, while she will guard her virtue intact. The symbolic association of the potion with the love of Cligés and Fénice is unusual (since the potion is in fact given to *Alis*), but its function as a means to preserve the possibility of their love establishes its relationship to their emotion even more definitely than did the gold hair for his parents.

Following these events, each story turns to scenes of war, battle, treachery, and—interspersed rhythmically in these—love. The correspondences among all these episodes (which I shall discuss below) are less precise in their physical arrangement and content, but equally exact in their analogical relationships and meaning, most of them involving dissimulation and concealment, or their opposites.

At this point, the work takes an unexpected structural turn, as Cligés, following the completion of the battles, decides that he must honor a promise made to his father and journey to Arthur's court. Such journeys have served as important pivots in Chrétien's work, as structural indications of a character's initiation into chivalry and love (although a love which so far the characters cannot admit or indulge). Clearly, Cligés's sojourn in Arthur's court marks a new beginning for him, and for more than one reason. First, of course, his father had assured him that a knight who has not been there cannot truly know prowess and valor (vss. 2565-70). But more important is the fact that, like most of the story of his parents, the progress of Cligés's and Fénice's love has until now been negligible. The impasse at which they find themselves is broken only after his return from England, although there was nothing in his trip (other than their longing for each other) to change their situation. Nonetheless, as his trip to Germany had preceded the discovery of love and the use of the magic potion, so do his journey and return lead to their finally admitting their love and determining to discover a way to indulge it. That way, of course, is by another potion, which will cause her apparent death. Here, the story resumes its correspondence with that of Alexandre;

whereas a messenger invents a lie concerning the latter's death, the death itself is "invented" in the case of Fénice. The truth is then learned in the first half and discovered by accident in the second, and those events are followed soon by the deaths, respectively, of Alexandre and Alis.

Thus, while the basic structural opposition of the poem is to be found in the two stories and characters (Alexandre and Cligés), we also find a rudimentary binary division within the second half itself. Cligés's return to Fénice corresponds generally to his initial meeting with her; in one scene they both experience love, and in the other they accept its inevitability and decide to do something about it. The two potions serve as structural doublets. And most of all, we find a contrast in their reactions before and after his journey to England. Until then, they may have recognized the love they feel and desired to express it, but under the circumstances, they responded no more definitely to their love than had Alexandre and Soredamors. Only after Cligés's return do they take the initiative and actively attempt to change the circumstances which militated against their love. Thus, the work really depicts three possible responses to love: Cligés's parents reject and combat it; he and Fénice admit it but at first offer no resistance to the obstacles in their way; finally, they reject their passive behavior and aggressively seek a solution.[14]

It may be useful to summarize in schematic form the structural relationships I have mentioned, although I shall omit from this summary the details of the central wars in each story.

Alexandre	Cligés (I)	Cligés (II)
Journey to Arthur's court	Journey to Germany	Journey to Arthur's court; return to Greece
Love discovered	Love discovered	Love admitted
Knighting	First battle	
Golden hair	First potion	Second potion
(war episodes)	(war episodes)	
Marriage; birth of Cligés		
Lie about Alexandre's death		Fénice's feigned death
Truth discovered		Truth discovered
Death of Alexandre		Death of Alis

Once we turn to the war scenes, we find that both the theme of the work and its bipartite division are reflected within the first half, which itself contains a similar division. Beginning with Angrés's sack of London, Chrétien presents two sections, almost identical in structure, in which there is a battle scene. Alexandre takes prisoners and is later rewarded by Arthur; a love scene follows. The single major distinction between these two portions of the narrative concerns the disposition of Alexandre's captives. The first time, he fears for their lives and thus delivers them to the queen. This angers Arthur, who consequently has them killed. Despite this cruel treatment, we later find Alexandre telling his prisoners to go and throw themselves on the king's mercy, for "tant est il dolz et deboneire" (vs. 2155) that he will not harm them—and in fact he does not. It is perhaps true, as Alexandre says (vss. 2140-41), that only the count has deserved to die, but nonetheless we cannot avoid the conclusion that Alexandre's conduct, developing from deception to forthrightness, provides a parallel to the same development between the first and second halves of the romance. Thus, even a description of the physical structure of *Cligés* leads us back to a consideration of the theme of the work.

Having established the opposition of concealment and revelation in the bipartite division of the first part of *Cligés*, Chrétien introduces that same motif, cast in numerous forms, into all parts of the work. The technique is very much like E.M. Forster's concept of rhythm in literature, which he defines as "repetition plus variation."[15] The motif, whether recalled by an episode or a single phrase, may be seen from the very beginning, but its structural and thematic significance becomes apparent only after we read further into the work.

From the first Alexandre is secretive, asking his father to promise him something unknown. Then, having extracted the promise, he explains that he wants to go to Arthur's court. Curiously, his behavior changes upon his arrival at court, and, far from being secretive, he announces immediately who he is and lives there for some time, spending and giving away money freely to win admiration. This contract between openness and secretiveness is repeated—but *reversed*—in the story of Alexandre's son. Cligés, too, wants to go to Arthur's court, but unlike his father he is open and honest, explaining where he wishes to go and asking his uncle's permission. Once there, however, his own behavior changes as he follows his father's advice that he conceal his identity at court until he has won the admiration of all the knights.

The actions of Cligés in Britain constitute the most extended elaboration of the concealment motif in the work. Learning that Arthur is holding his court at Oxford, he goes there and engages in tourneys on four successive days, wearing armor of a different color each day and hiding himself at night. Only after he has inspired the awe and admiration of all the others does he relent and reveal his identity.

Thus, Alexandre's reticence and his concealment of love are emphasized ironically by the extreme openness and generosity which he demonstrates at court, whereas Cligés's forthrightness toward his uncle and Fénice stands in contrast with the secretiveness which Alexandre had advised him to show in Britain. The characters' attitudes and actions merely underline the tragic fact that the love Cligés and Fénice feel and admit readily is, as I have indicated above, an impossible love.

The author's play on the contrast of concealment and revelation continues throughout the work and can be observed, not only in most of the major episodes, but in relatively insignificant details as well. We see the pattern reflected in such episodes as that in which the treacherous followers of Angrés decide to attack Arthur's camp concealed by the darkness of the night. However, as Chrétien points out, God hates traitors and treachery and thus causes the moon to shine on their shields and helmets, revealing their presence to Arthur's men (vss. 1672-90). The ensuing battle scene contains a further exposition of the pattern, for Alexandre proposes that they disguise themselves with the dead traitors' equipment (vss. 1815-28). In this way, they succeed in entering the town gates and taking the enemy by surprise. Later, Cligés will use this same ploy, appropriating an enemy's helmet, shield, and horse, and revealing his identity only when he has taken the Saxons unawares (vss. 3462-3528).

The first of these two disguise scenes provides us with the best illustration of Chrétien's technique of using an incidental reference, sometimes a single word,[16] to foreshadow a theme which he will later develop fully. After Alexandre and his men have disguised themselves, the Greeks find their equipment left beside the enemies' bodies and suppose their compatriots to be dead. Chrétien remarks, almost as an aside, that they were

> . . . con cil qui songe,
> Qui por verité croit mançonge,
> Les boisent li escu boclé,
> Car la mançonge font verté.
>
> (vss. 2073-76)

The simile which Chrétien uses in referring to the disguise scene can only be an obvious, if casual, foreshadowing of Thessala's magic potion which makes Alis dream of making love to Fénice and take his dream to be true. Even the language is similar, for Thessala will say of the Emperor:

> Di li avra joie a talant,
> Et cuidera tot antresait

Que an veillant sa joie an ait,
Et ja rien n'en tenra a songe
A losange ne a mançonge.

(vss. 3168-72)

The potion works, "et si tendra le songe a voir" (vs. 3304).

The essential episodes of *Cligés* are of course this one, in which the magic potion preserves Fénice's virginity for Cligés, and the later one concerning a potion which causes her apparent death and permits her to be united with the one she loves. In both cases, the episodes involve the effect of a potion, but more to the point, both the potions serve to conceal a situation from the emperor and his people, thereby continuing the theme established from the beginning of the romance.

Only after the convenient death of Alis can Cligés and Fénice express their love openly. Significantly, Fénice's concern throughout has not been for her virtue or for Christian concepts of morality; she wants to protect not her virginity but her reputation, and she even distorts the advice of St. Paul to justify her conviction:

"Ja avoec vos ensi n'irai,
Car lors seroit par tot le monde
Ausi come d'Ysolt la Blonde
Et de Tristant de nos parlé;
Quant nos an serïens alé,
Et ci, et la, totes et tuit
Blasmeroient nostre deduit.
Nus ne diroit, ne devroit croirre
La chose si com ele est voire.
De vostre oncle qui crerroit dons
Que je si li fusse an pardons
Pucele estorse et eschapee?
Por trop baude et trop estapee
Me tendroit l'en, et vos por fol.
Mes le comandemant saint Pol
Fet boen garder et retenir:
Qui chaste ne se vialt tenir,
Sainz Pos a feire bien anseingne
Si sagement que il n'an preingne
Ne cri, ne blasme, ne reproche.

(vss. 5250-69)

If their actions were morally or religiously motivated, they could no more admit their love to themselves and each other than they could flaunt it before others. As it is, they can accept it, but others must not know, and this contrast provides the basis for the opposition of concealment and revelation. The secretiveness practiced by Alexandre and Soredamors is *forced* upon Cligés and Fénice, and in addition to hiding their love from others, they also conceal her chastity from Alis. And the essential and final irony of the work is the fact that they are forced to conceal Fénice's very existence from others, by having her feign death and then hide in a secret tower in order to enjoy the love they recognize and welcome so readily.

A discussion of the form of *Cligés* must obviously make a distinction between a physical (external) structure and a thematic (internal) structure. In its external form, *Cligés* is as loosely constructed as possible, its only unifying narrative element being the son's following the father's example in leaving Greece to seek renown and glory at Arthur's court. On the other hand, Chrétien *has* succeeded in unifying the work by introducing narrative patterns which reflect the opposition of concealment and revelation— the reactions, respectively, of Alexandre and Cligés to love.

It is apparent that the pattern I have discussed can recur in contexts having only an incidental thematic significance in the work. This pattern is established in the principal episodes (where it *does* have a direct and obvious thematic importance) and reflected in a variety of forms in other parts of the romance, where its significance is basically structural: it relates peripheral episodes to the central ones, and details to the whole, to organize a complex and disparate narrative into a unified poem.

Lancelot

As in the case of the other romances, the structural question which has received perhaps the most attention in regard to the *Charrette* is the number of natural divisions of the work. The question is both important and intriguing, but whether the work is tripartite, as Kelly suggests (*Charrette*, p. 184), or whether it is thematically bipartite and structurally tripartite, as Zaddy indicates (pp. 117-18)—or has five, or some other number of parts—the disagreements suggest more than anything else that the poem, like most of Chrétien's others (and, indeed, like literary works in general), is multistructural. Depending on the critic's point of view, different episodes will assume structural significance and permit us to construct different but equally valid formal analyses. In the *Charrette*, the importance attached, for example, to the cart scene or to the quest for Gauvain will profoundly influence the results of our study. In addition, I suspect that critics not only differ with each other in the choice of episodes to which they attach particular importance, but there is also the possibility that with a modern perspective they may also disagree with the author. For example, in a work like *Cligés*, we would no doubt tend to view the discovery or admission of love, or perhaps the false death scene, as the episode possessing the greatest thematic significance. Yet, the episode given particular prominence by its position in the exact center of the work is rather the potion given, not to Fénice, but to her husband. That potion is the instrument by which she, who already knows she loves Cligés and desires to preserve her virtue, manages to do so. Clearly, in the narrative development of the work, that is as important as the discovery of love, and in fact, as a solution to a problem it is fully as important as the situation which required it. Structurally, the profession of love *may* be the central event of the *Charrette*; not so for *Cligés*.

The centrality of episodes and their organization into patterns appear to me to be of primary importance, and I can do no better here than refer to Douglas Kelly's very detailed analysis of the *Charrette*.[17] First of all, his contention that the work is tripartite is supported by the numerous tripartite subdivisions within sections, and while that finding is obviously susceptible to the same subjective selection I mentioned above, I find the reflection of the poem's divisions in those of its various components to be a persuasive argument for tripartition. Moreover, according to Kelly (p. 184):

> ... the poem is built upon a symmetrical pattern, with the scene in which Lancelot and Guenevere confess and analyze their love as the core. This episode is found in the center of the central structural division (B) of the plot which describes the events that took place in Bath. Embracing the central division are the two divisions describing Lancelot's quest (A) and Lancelot's imprisonment (C); they contribute to the symmetry of the plan by their respective positions directly before and after the central division as well as by the similarity of their internal tripartite structure. The opening and closing Arthurian scenes complete the symmetrical arrangement while serving as nouement and denouement to the plot.

I consider it unnecessary to present a further analysis of the physical structure of the poem, for it would duplicate many of Kelly's ideas and conclusions. Nonetheless, there remain additional questions of form, and particularly of the poem's "inner structure," and the relation of its meaning to the structure. The principle by which Chrétien fixes and elaborates that relationship is, once again, the analogical reflection of the central theme or intrigue of the poem in numerous other episodes and sub-themes.

Like most of Chrétien's heroes, Lancelot commits an offense which he must expiate at length and with great difficulty. The significant fact is that the events used in the expiation episodes reflect in a variety of ways both the nature and the form of the offense. Lancelot's offense is his hesitation to humiliate himself by getting into the cart; in other words, his shame is his hesitation to *accept* shame for love's sake. There is a precise correspondence between this act and his later willingness (at the Noauz tourney: vss. 5652-76, 5852-67) to humiliate himself without a second thought to please the queen. The question of hesitation is as important as that of humiliation. These two motifs, which perfectly relate the final expiation to the offense, are reflected in all parts of the work; hesitation in particular seems to be structurally significant. The first pertinent example is the episode of the flaming lance (vss. 503-04), when Gauvain lies in the bed designated for him, whereas Lancelot without hesitation chooses the bed forbidden to him. This episode appears to be only peripherally related to the quest, but it is thematically attached to it as soon as the poet points out Lancelot's refusal to delay a choice and his tendency to choose the difficult way. A similar case, but one which is thematically more prominent and which elucidates the preceding one, is the choice which must be made between the sword-bridge and the water-bridge (vss. 645-99). Both ways are perilous, but the sword-bridge is both shorter and more dangerous. By this time, it is no surprise that Gauvain chooses the longer but less dangerous, whereas Lancelot readily undertakes the more dangerous way in order to arrive sooner at his destination. Later, a knight suggests a safer route to the bridge, but Lancelot, who seeks the most direct way (vss. 2151-53), learns again that the safer route is also longer and immediately chooses the shorter one. Despite the dangers he may face, delay is unconscionable to the knight whose quest was necessitated, in the cart scene, by a tragic delay.

A still better example of Chrétien's technique is offered by Lancelot's experiences with the lady whose offer of lodging is contingent on his agreeing to sleep with her (vss. 931-1280). This episode provides a double parallel to the central problem of the work. After dining, Lancelot leaves the hall to wait for the time to rejoin her. He returns to find that during this wait she has disappeared. He has, in a sense, "lost her," and he vows that, wherever she may be, he will look for her until he finds her (vss. 1054-55). When he does find her being mistreated by another knight (in the presence of six armed guards), he *hesitates* to defend her and pronounces a monologue which, significantly, might have been his reasoning in the cart episode:

. . .Dex, que porrai ge feire?
Meüz sui por si grant afeire
Con por la reïne Guenievre.
Ne doi mie avoir cuer de lievre

Quant por li sui an ceste queste:
Se Malvestiez son cuer me preste
E je son comandemant faz,
N'ateindrai pas ce que je chaz;
Honiz sui se je ci remaing.
Molt me vient or a grant desdaing,
Quant j'ai parlé del remenoir;
Molt en ai le cuer triste et noir;
Or en ai honte, or en ai duel
Tel que je morroie mon vuel
Quant je ai tant demoré ci.

(vss. 1097-1111)

These events turn out, notably, to be a test. Yet, while he considers whether to delay his quest for Guenevere by defending this lady, his actions constitute a delay in his immediate duty to the latter, and this episode is thus transformed into an analogue of his original hesitation regarding the queen.

The dual motifs of humiliation and hesitation are worked into a series of miscellaneous episodes involving Lancelot's battles. In the first one (vss. 730-930) he is fighting with the guard of the ford; the combat continues for some time, until Lancelot is ashamed to have taken so long to defeat a single knight. He presses and gains the victory. Later, in a similar situation, Lancelot blames and reproaches himself for such a delay, because the spectators have seen him unable to defeat his adversary; then he is again successful (vss. 2677-2778). This scene recalls the former one, and they both exploit the delay motif, but they derive their main significance from the fact that they foreshadow later episodes in which the general situation will be repeated in the presence of Guenevere. During the long battle with Meleagant (vss. 3536-3817), neither knight has the advantage until a maiden indicates to Lancelot that Guenevere is watching the battle. We would then expect him to win, but the sight of the queen distracts him, and he defends himself with backhand blows until he is told to turn so that he faces both the queen and his adversary. He then attacks so fiercely that Guenevere agrees to ask him to cease the battle. Lancelot hears her and immediately desists, because

Molt est qui aimme obeïssanz,
Et molt fet tost et volentiers,
La ou il est amis antiers,
Ce qu'a s'amie doie plaire.

(vss. 3798-3801)

This is a pivotal scene because it reflects the two earlier ones, it is duplicated in the next battle with Meleagant (vss. 4987-5025), and it also foreshadows two later scenes—at the tourney—in which for a different reason Guenevere will command him, not to cease fighting, but to fight his worst. These tourney episodes are the conclusion of a long series of battles related not by sequence but by similarity, with each one containing some element which recalls the preceding one to the reader's mind. Moreover, these scenes represent the conclusion of the quest and the reuniting of the two principal motifs: in contrast to the scene of the cart, Lancelot now demonstrates that he will, *without hesitation*, accept the worst possible humiliation for the sake of his love. In other words, love is now more important than pride, and Guenevere more than himself.

There still remain a number of other episodes which offer analogies to the poem's major themes.[18] For instance, the work contains several scenes in which Lancelot promises his affection to another. I have already referred to the lady whose offer of lodging he accepts with regret, since it requires his agreeing to sleep with her. Later, a seneschal's wife agrees to release him from his prison, to attend the tourney, if he will return and then give her his love (vss. 5446-94). Like the previous adventure, this one involves a test of Lancelot. Finally, we see Lancelot imprisoned in a tower, and he laments the notable fact that Gauvain has delayed too long in coming to his aid (vss. 6483-99). Then the daughter of Bademagu helps him escape, after he has offered to serve her forever. The physical and thematic similarity of these scenes is obvious, but equally significant is the progression in his willingness to take any action necessary to fulfill his duty. In the first episode, he hesitates, then agrees because he can see no alternative; in the second he accepts the lady's offer without hesitation; finally, it is Lancelot himself who takes the initiative in order to gain his temporary freedom. Thus, as he first hesitates in his duty to Guenevere and finally obeys her without hesitation, the progress of his quest is indicated in this series of episodes by his development from reluctance to willingness to eagerness. Moreover, just as he has to learn to accept humiliation to atone for his desire to avoid it, he also has to be willing to give his love to another in order to gain that of Guenevere. Such paradoxical situations provide much of the dramatic tension of Chrétien's poems.

Thus far, all the episodes I have discussed have presented analogies to the subjects of delay and disgrace; yet the *Charrette* deals extensively with at least one additional motif. The poem is very much about perception in all its forms, from physical vision to the misinterpretation of phenomena. These subjects are organized into a secondary structural system which runs parallel to the principal one. It is from this point of view that the work is more complex than Chrétien's other romances: not because episodes are numerous or complicated, but because the poet applies his analogical technique of composition to two separate systems.

The *Charrette* is in fact the most "visual" of Chrétien's poems; it is difficult to turn a page without finding references to visual matters— to the things characters see, to the angle of view, to windows and other frames for the action. Of greater thematic significance is a recurrent motif which I have mentioned earlier: the faulty interpretation of perceived phenomena. The scene which establishes its importance is the cart scene itself. In the *Charrette*, it is no longer true that a knight must avoid anything which will bring him shame, and Lancelot thus misinterprets the meaning of the cart, as do those who reproach his riding in it. Once established, this pattern generates its own structural analogies, such as the scene in which Keu is blamed for the blood on Guenevere's bed. Incidental echoes of the misinterpretation motif occur in scenes such as those involving false rumors of the deaths of Lancelot and Guenevere.

There are thus two organizing systems in the poem. The relationship of the second (involving perception) to the theme of the work is less than entirely clear, although it is nevertheless effective as an organizing technique. It does, as I pointed out in an earlier chapter, serve to establish the distance between author and text necessary to prevent their identification with each other. Structurally, however, Chrétien is at his best in the elaboration of the hesitation and humiliation patterns, where there is a perfect correspondence between meaning and form. The narrative material of the *Charrette* is complex, but Chrétien's method relates scene to scene to hold it together in a simultaneous structure. The result is a perplexing but intriguing romance, and an excellent representative of the genre.

Yvain

Although there has been considerable disagreement concerning the organization of *Yvain* (again, whether it contains two or three sections, or more), few critics have been disposed to deny that this work is the best constructed of Chrétien's romances. In fact, such a judgment is frequently offered without qualification: "*Yvain*, le mieux construit des romans de Chrétien . . ." (Zumthor, *Essai*, p. 481); Frappier is only slightly less categorical: "*Yvain* est, avec *Erec*, le roman le mieux construit de Chrétien."[19] In contrast to most other medieval romances, this poem does indeed possess a simplicity and clarity of form which we would be likely to call "classic" if that term did not have more precise historical applications. But despite this clarity and the somewhat reduced number of episodes comprising the actual quest,[20] it will be useful for us to examine the relationships existing among episodes and (as in the other romances) between the form of the work and its meaning.

Yvain follows the general pattern of Chrétien's works, in that the hero is required to perform a series of difficult or heroic acts to make reparation for an error which he has committed. Thus, despite his promise, Yvain permits his quest for adventure to delay his return to his wife, Laudine, whose love consequently turns to hate. After a period of madness, of which a lady cures him with a magic ointment, he saves the life of a lion attacked by a serpent, and he undertakes five adventures in defense of maidens who are endangered or enslaved. Eventually, he is successful in regaining Laudine's love.

As I suggested, few critics would now agree with the contention that this portion of the work presented a number of disconnected episodes, without meaning or structure, strung together for the pure amusement of the reader.[21] It has become quite clear to most readers that the last part of the poem traces Yvain's moral ascension; that is, his evolution to the point where he is once again deserving of Laudine's love. Furthermore, Chrétien is careful to establish an order and a progression (from less to greater difficulty and from greater to less self-interest on Yvain's part) among the episodes. Yet a careful reading of the work reveals a further coherence created by the internal connections among the characters. A detailed examination of this section will demonstrate the existence of an intricate and precisely balanced structure which must be counted among the most remarkable of Chrétien's achievements.[22]

On the most elementary level, the structure of Yvain's exploits consists of a simple and precise interlace of episodes; that is, the poet interrupts an event and postpones its conclusion in order to recount another story. Thus Yvain, having pledged his aid to Lunete, is asked in the meantime to fight Harpin de la Montagne, an undertaking which very nearly prevents his arriving in time to save her. Similarly, having later agreed to defend the rights of the younger daughter of the Seigneur de la Noire Espine, he interrupts his return to court in order to deliver three hundred maidens— the *tisseuses*—from their oppression in the Castle of Pesme Avanture. This interlacing clearly organizes the adventures into a symmetrical pattern; the question is whether it is anything more than a purely mechanical arrangement of episodes. Frappier does indicate that the technique serves to "piquer la curiosité," thus contributing to the creation of dramatic tension.[23] But, in addition, I suggest that it reflects and develops in a precise way the central theme of the *roman*. It will be recalled that, immediately after Yvain's marriage, Gauvain, typifying the knight who pursues adventure for its own sake, urges his friend to leave with him in search of excitement and glory; he tells Yvain that a knight must not permit his worth and valor to decrease when he marries. Promising Laudine that he will return within a year, Yvain leaves with Gauvain, but his preoccupation with adventure causes him to forget his obligation. He overstays the year's leave, and Laudine sends a messenger to inform him that he has betrayed her and that, as a result, he has destroyed the love she had for him.

There is, in the principle I have designated as Chrétien's *contrappasso*, a parallel between these episodes and those which recount the expiation. Once Yvain disregards a promise or obligation which he had freely contracted, he is twice confronted with situations which threaten to distract him from other obligations. The two interpolated episodes (Gauvain's relatives and the three hundred maidens) thus provide a sort of test of Yvain's constancy and resolve, and the expiation involves not simply the performance of noble acts, but his determination not to be diverted, even by the most worthy of causes, from the fulfillment of his obligations. We might expect Yvain to be facing the most agonizing dilemma when he has to decide between the defense of Lunete and that of his best friend's relatives, but whatever personal agony he may feel is subordinated without question to the moral urgency which dictates his decision. Fortunately, the timely arrival of Harpin spares him the decision by permitting him to defend both causes, but he has already declared, in an unmistakable recollection of his earlier *folie*, that if he cannot return in time to aid Lunete, he will either die or take leave of his senses:

Sa vie avroit corte duree
Ou il istroit toz vis del sens
S'il n'i pooit venir a tens.

(vss. 4074-76)

In summary, the episodes in which an interpolation into an event threatens to delay its resolution reflect the precise manner in which Yvain's wandering with Gauvain interrupts his marriage and distracts him from his promise to return with a year. We may, then, consider that the *roman* contains not two, but *three*, pairs of interlaced episodes. Three times Yvain has an obligation to a lady (Laudine, Lunete, and the younger sister), and three times his attention is diverted to another undertaking (the exploits with Gauvain, the defense of Gauvain's relatives, and the liberation of the *tisseuses*). It is this reflection of the central intrigue in the events that follow which gives significance to the interlace; while recounting the expiation, the poet twice repeats the narrative pattern which he has chosen for the offense, the only difference being that Yvain is determined not to repeat the offense itself.

At this point the role of Gauvain merits closer attention, for his part in the work does not end with his persuading Yvain to leave his wife. Although Gauvain plays no direct part in the action between his wandering with Yvain and their combat, Chrétien takes care to keep him before the reader's eyes throughout much of the *roman.*

From the moment he first meets Lunete at Yvain's wedding he loves her; and he claims her as his lady. Significantly, he contracts an obligation which may be considered a general parallel of Yvain's marriage vows, when he tells her that she will be his *dameisele,* and he will be her knight, to help her when she needs him. Yet when her life is later threatened, she laments that only Gauvain and Yvain could save her and that Gauvain has gone in search of Queen Guenevere, whom an unknown knight has taken away from the court. It is this same quest which prevents Gauvain from coming to the defense of his own relatives, threatened by Harpin de la Montagne. When in his stead Yvain defeats Harpin, he asks nothing, except that Gauvain be told of his exploits. And of course, Yvain's final combat is with Gauvain himself.

Thus, during the expiation episodes, Gauvain stands in direct opposition to the hero, as he does in the *Chevalier de la charrette* and the *Conte del graal.* His precise function here is easily understood: he serves as a constant reminder of Yvain's offense. First, it is he who persuades Yvain to leave Laudine, and he comes to represent, as I have suggested, the love of adventure and the pure pleasure of its pursuit. But in addition, Gauvain's experiences reflect his friend's fault in a more precise way, for he, like Yvain, forgets his obligations. He owes allegiance both to Lunete and to his own relatives; yet when they need him he is occupied in another adventure. Each time Yvain undertakes the task for him. There is no doubt that in seeking to rescue the Queen, Gauvain is performing a noble service, but in so doing, he is denying his aid to others who deserve and expect it. Without condemning Gauvain's quest, Chrétien calls attention to his frivolous nature, in order to remind the reader that this had been Yvain's failing. This contrapuntal effect makes of Gauvain's role an important part of the work. Having established a motif or pattern (distraction from an obligation) in the episode of Yvain's offense, Chrétien uses variations of that pattern both to recount its expiation and to reflect the offense itself in Gauvain's acts.

In contrast to Yvain, Gauvain undergoes no evolution during the work; he is at the beginning a valiant knight, and that is what he remains. Since Yvain's madness the two friends have represented different ideals— simple adventure on the one hand, love and devotion on the other. The divergence between the character of the knights becomes progressively wider, until finally they come into direct conflict with one another, for Gauvain is the older sister's champion.[24] The fact that Gauvain is carefully kept before our eyes and that his actions are contrasted to those of Yvain suggests that Chrétien intends for us to see in the battle of these two men the opposition of the two ideals. Significantly, neither is able to gain a victory; yet the outcome, a reconciliation rather than a simple stalemate, appears to reflect Chrétien's answer to the problem which the work poses—the conflict between knightly prowess and love. As in *Erec et Enide* the hero had abandoned adventure for love, Yvain had abandoned love for adventure. The knightly ideal is obviously the reconciliation of the two forces. Whereas Gauvain seeks adventure for its own sake, the knight who now identifies himself as the *chevalier au lion* comes finally to represent adventure undertaken for a cause; namely, the service of women and love. Love, spurring him to more noble and valiant efforts, makes of Yvain a hero, whose worth and renown effect the eventual reconciliation with Laudine.

Thus far I have spoken of the episodes of the two sisters and of the *tisseuses* only in general terms. Structurally, the *entrelacement* of these adventures simply duplicates that of the earlier ones: the defense of the three hundred maidens interrupts Yvain's journey back to the court to defend the rights of the younger sister. The difference is that Yvain is no longer performing services because of personal obligations or desires, and for this reason the significance of these last two events is not immediately apparent;[25] yet they are a necessary and organic part of the *roman*. Admittedly, these episodes appear to have little or nothing to do with those which precede them or with Yvain's situation, but I think that very fact provides their justification. As Yvain develops morally, we see a progression, not only toward more difficult combats, but also toward more gratuitous acts. First of all he repays an immediate and personal debt to the lady who has just saved his life and cured his madness. Next he undertakes to repay a debt to Lunete, his friend and ally who had persuaded Laudine to marry him. To this point Yvain has strong personal reasons for his actions, as he does to almost the same extent when he next defends the relatives of his friend Gauvain. By way of contrast the final pair of adventures are acts in defense of unknown maidens in distress. In the case of the *tisseuses*, there is pressure brought on Yvain to do battle, but in the final episode his defense of the disinherited sister is undertaken freely, out of charity and pity. There are thus two distinct stages in Yvain's evolution: first, he must prove himself capable of fulfilling his obligations, for he had erred in not doing so, but only by performing actions in which he has no personal stake or interest beyond increasing his worth does he show his moral ascension to be complete.

In conclusion, the latter part of *Yvain* could not differ more from Paris's description of a formless series of episodes. Framed between Yvain's first visit to the magic fountain, after which he met and married Laudine, and the last, bringing about their reconciliation, the section includes not only the mechanical symmetry of the interlaced adventures but the parallel of each pair of adventures to the central episode of the work. In addition, there is the moral ascension of Yvain, who at first, with Gauvain, seeks adventure for amusement, who next accepts it to repay personal debts, and who finally performs acts of pure chivalry and mercy. And throughout there is the figure of Gauvain to remind Yvain of his former self and by the final reconciliation to affirm the validity—for Chrétien—of responsible action, of adventure in the service of love.

The remarkable fact about the narrative configuration of the episodes of Yvain's expiation is the precise, almost "organic," way they relate themselves to the main situation of the work—by form, function, meaning, and content. Yet we do not have to look far to find a number of other episodes in the poem which reflect the central theme without establishing any causal (or other) connection between them. It will suffice to point out here two of the more prominent among such scenes.

The first occurs at the very beginning of the romance, when without reason or explanation Arthur lingers too long in the Queen's chamber and falls asleep. This, Chrétien remarks, is unusual behavior for the king, and it is behavior not to be overlooked by the other knights, who become impatient and begin to grumble: "Si ot de tex cui molt greva/Et qui molt grant parole an firent" (vss. 44-45). Outside the chamber door, Calogrenant begins to tell of an adventure which once befell him, and when the queen comes out to listen, nothing more is said of Arthur until the tale is told. At that point, he awakens, joins them, and hears the story retold by the queen, but the subject of his unaccustomed neglect of his court on a feastday is never mentioned again. Indeed, there is no need to mention it further, for it has nothing whatsoever to do with the subsequent development of the story. Yet, if we recall that Gauvain will caution Yvain against remaining long with his wife, the initial scene appears to be a loose and distant prefiguration of the hero's situation (an inverted prefiguration, to be sure, since Yvain does leave his wife). The two situations are in no way related, and the first one is of no real importance to the narrative; it does, however, acquire meaning of another kind, as a casual reflection of a pattern established in the central intrigue of the poem.

The most fascinating of these "casual" analogues occurs as part of the adventures of Calogrenant. Within the story which he tells at court, we find the details of his relationship with a hospitable vavasor and his beautiful daughter. They give him lodging, and at their invitation he promises to return soon. He proceeds to the fountain, where he meets his disgraceful defeat. On his way back he remembers his promise:

En la fin, volantez me vint
Qu'a mon oste covant tanroie
Et que a lui m'an revanroie.
Ensi me plot, ensi le fis
Mes jus totes mes armes mis
Por plus aler legieremant,
Si m'an reving honteusemant.

(vss. 554-60)

The details of this event may well be, *within the context of his adventures*, the least significant portion of the story, and yet they present another parallel to the hero of the work. Calogrenant failed in his adventure; Yvain will succeed. But it is important to note also that, despite his shame, Calogrenant was able to forget the damage his reputation had suffered in order to do what he had promised. It will be precisely Yvain's concern for his reputation which will *prevent* him from doing the same and will cause him to lose the love of Laudine. Moreover, and again despite his shame, Calogrenant is received no less hospitably upon his return than he had been earlier:

Onques de rien ne m'aparçui
Ne de sa fille ne de lui,
Que moins volentiers me veïssent
Ne que moins d'enor me feïssent
Qu'il avoient fet l'autre nuit.

(vss. 565-69)

The lesson here, which is given in an understated manner, is that, contrary to Gauvain's assurances, hospitality, respect, and presumably love depend less on reputation than on character. Yvain lost his wife's heart through his search for the fame he thought would win it. Thus, while Yvain sets out immediately to right the wrong done to Calogrenant's reputation, there is within the experiences of the latter a suggestion, or prefiguration, of the problem which will lead to disaster for the hero. Such reflections serve to impart to the work the feeling that nothing happens which is not somehow related to the hero's situation. Nothing in that chivalric world is without significance, and nothing in the author's literary world is ultimately as gratuitous as the episodic narrative organization might lead us to think.

Perceval

In his study of Chrétien's *Conte del Graal*, Frappier notes that the interpretation of this romance ". . . sera toujours difficile et en partie problématique, à la fois en raison de son symbolisme et de son ina- chèvement."[26] Some critics, in addition, have long been disturbed by the apparent duality of the work: at line 4747 the story of Perceval is suddenly interrupted, and the remainder of the poem, except for the some three hundred lines of the hermit scene, is devoted instead to Gauvain's adventures. As a result, Hoepffner and others accepted the idea that we have in *Perceval* two distinct works, joined by a clumsy "editor" after Chrétien's death. This problem should not detain us for long, for, as Frappier indicates, Chrétien had already used such a dual exposition in *Cligés*, relating the story of the father before beginning that of the son.

Nor, of course, is it unusual for Chrétien to offer the adventures of Gauvain as a parallel or counterpoise to those of the hero. We have seen Gauvain play that role in *Lancelot* and *Yvain*, and he obviously serves a similar purpose in *Perceval*. In all three of these romances, he is a static character: whatever else may change, he goes on as always, doing the same things for the same reasons. He thus serves as a chivalrous model for Perceval, but he is a model to be surpassed. Moreover, we easily discover a rather precise system of thematic and structural corre- spondences which link the second part of the work to the first. A single example will suffice: the episode of the *pucele as mances petites* (see vss. 4983 ff.), struck by her sister for her defense of Gauvain, is an obvious reflection of the scene in which Kay had cruelly struck the smiling maiden who had spoken well of Perceval. Further examples would simply confirm the opinions of most recent critics, who agree that the text which we have is a large fragment of a single romance, which possesses a remarkable degree of unity despite its unfinished state.[27]

Traditionally, *Perceval* is considered a *Bildungsroman*: the story of a naive and ignorant youth who is initiated successively into chivalry, love, and finally religion and who thus passes from a human level to a moral and almost divine level. He begins at zero and ends as the elect, the knight who, the work implies, will seek and find the Grail. According to Frappier, for example, we see in the sequence of episodes an evident gradation, and in the character of the hero a progressive development, and the majority of critics would no doubt accept such a judgment. Among those who deny that such an evolution occurs, we must count first Peter Haidu, for whom any idea of progression would be illusory. In his opinion, Perceval accumulates knowledge of the world and acquires a mastery of the chivalric craft, but his flaws of understanding go without remedy; that is, he becomes more and more capable in a worldly sense but undergoes no moral evolution. Haidu's theory is appealing as an explanation of the comedy and irony which inform the work, but it does not seem to recognize that the romance can be read *at the same time* as a masterpiece of irony and comedy *and* as the story of the moral transformation of Perceval. Whatever may be the climate which dominates the story up to the Grail Castle scene, the final episodes of Perceval's story (and in particular the hermit scene) point to a moral ascension on his part and argue for at least a qualified acceptance of Frappier's evolutionary interpretation.

We can distinguish in Perceval's adventures three principal stages or movements (in addition to his initial—primitive or natural—state). At the beginning of the work, when he makes his first contact with the world outside his mother's forest, he is confronted by situations which would normally require a worldly and cultivated response. He however knows nothing of the world, and his limited understanding leads him to imprint on all these situations a religious interpretation. Thus, his mother having told him that devils are the most frightening and angels the most beautiful of creatures, he considers the knights to be the former (because of the sound their approach makes) and then as the latter (by their appearance). Later, after leaving his mother, he comes to a tent, which he assumes to be the edifice which his mother had described to him and to which she had given the name "church."

In the central part of the story, the intrigue requires not only knowledge and chivalrous talents but, above all, certain judgments of an essentially moral order which go against the code Perceval has accepted. It is notably in the Grail Castle that this opposition of his moral responsibility to the precepts of chivalry is developed with great clarity. If he had permitted himself to act on instinct, he would have asked the Grail question, but Chrétien tells us that, despite his curiosity, Perceval remembers the advice given him by Gornemant, and, eager to be a proper knight, he remains silent. From this point of view, then, the second section of the work represents an inversion of the first. While the narrative moves from the worldly to the moral or religious, Perceval himself evolves in the opposite direction. This sort of inversion, as we have seen elsewhere, is scarcely a novelty for Chrétien, and this opposition of the thesis with Perceval's antithesis implies a further development.

That development, which the unfinished state of the work prevents our confirming, would presumably be a higher state of consciousness on the part of Perceval, who would resolutely use his physical and chivalrous talents in the cause of a religious ideal, the quest of the Grail. Without such an evolution, he would be unable to complete the quest, and indeed, he would not have undertaken it with the urgency he shows when Gauvain and the others decide to seek certain adventures but he *redit tot el* and sets out to find the Grail.

There have been several attempts to define the structure of Perceval's story; two of these will interest us here. The first is the analysis made by Süheyla Bayrav,[28] who divides the Perceval text into two broad divisions, with the Grail Castle scene occupying the central position and serving as a dividing line. Episodes in the first part correspond to those of the second, as follows: the encounter with the knights at the beginning corresponds to his encounter with his cousin after he leaves the Grail Castle; in the first he learns of his chivalric vocation, while the second depicts the discovery of his fault and his identity. Next, his brutality to the Tent Maiden corresponds, quite obviously, to his defense of her. Symbolic meanings then link the Red Knight episode to the three drops of blood in the snow. Gornemant's instruction scene corresponds to that of the hideous damsel who rebukes Perceval and reminds him of his duties. Finally, his awakening to love in the Blancheflor episode is related structurally to the closing of his heart during his five years of wandering.

I will dispense with a detailed critique of Bayrav's analysis, although such a critique might deal with such questions as the tenuous bases for certain of her associations. The images of redness, for example, certainly provide a distant (and perhaps vague) link between the Red Knight scene and that of the three drops of blood, but do the episodes *function* the same way? I do not think so. And in any case, why does the latter scene not call to mind instead the single drop of blood at the lance's point? The color there too is set off by the whiteness of the weapon's shaft. Despite a number of possible objections, nonetheless, Bayrav's system does conserve, as I think any such analysis must, the central place given, structurally and thematically, to the Grail Castle events.

Stanton de V. Hoffman, in response to Bayrav's study, has proposed for the work a tripartite structure:[29] "There are then three broad sections of the Perceval plot of the *Conte del Graal*, and they involve three restorations, three advices, and three quests." His divisions are as follows:

Part I	Mother's advice Restoration of Arthur's cup	Quest of chivalry, of knighthood and of Arthur's court (as Perceval speaks of his mother's advice)
Part II	Gornemant's advice Restoration of Blancheflor's kingdom	Quest of his mother (as he speaks of Gornemant's advice)
Part III	Hermit's advice Restoration of the Grail Castle	Quest of the Grail (twice interrupted)

Despite its generality—or no doubt because of it—this analysis presents fewer problems and has the virtue of emphasizing the triple quest structure and, correspondingly, the three scenes in which advice is given. Of course, Perceval fails at his first opportunity to restore the Grail Castle and its King, and the critic must infer his final success (an inference which appears reasonable but must be made with caution). Taking Hoffman's suggestions as a sound point of departure, we may go a bit further than either he or Bayrav into an analysis of the structure of the Perceval sequence.

Chrétien has framed the hero's adventures between two episodes which are rather obvious analogues of each other: the first scene, the beginning, in his mother's forest, and the final hermit scene, a "new beginning" in another forest.[30] Not only the setting but also the content and meaning of the first scene are reflected in the hermit episode. Both represent an awakening on Perceval's part, the first time to chivalry itself and then later to religion. Furthermore, the awakening is accompanied by his persistent questions, which appear almost as naive and uninformed in the particular context of the Good Friday scene as they had earlier, when he first met the knights in his mother's forest. Finally, he asks directions in each instance and finds his way to King Arthur and to the holy hermit, respectively.

Between these two episodes, a secondary frame is provided by Perceval's two visits to Arthur's court, the first time as a nameless and naive youth, the second as a distinguished and admired practitioner of the chivalric craft. As we will see, the symmetry of the work's form is approximate rather than exact, for the Tent Maiden scene which precedes his first arrival at the court and the scene of the Hideous Maiden who causes him to leave court, in the later episode, are not functionally equivalent. Nonetheless, there is a general organization of the work around the central episode (the Grail Castle sequence and the explanation of its meaning by Perceval's cousin, two events which I see as inseparable); thus, Perceval's liberation of Blancheflor and his liberation of the Tent Maiden mirror one another and serve as a frame around the center of the Perceval-plot.

If we go further in our analysis, we find striking and systematic parallels among episodes (although, as I suggested, we may be disappointed by the imperfect nature of some correspondences). Thus, although I agree with Hoffman that Perceval himself undertakes three quests, the text presents four of them in all. At the beginning, the hero is seeking Arthur and chivalric fulfillment; then, beginning with his departure from Gornemant, he is seeking his mother. But after the Grail Castle debacle, while Perceval is wandering rather aimlessly, it is Arthur who undertakes a quest, determined (in a loose parallel both to Perceval's earlier failure and his later mission) to find the hero and pose a question which he had earlier left unasked (Perceval's name). The hero's third quest, but the poem's fourth, is to be the Grail quest.

These four movements seem to me rather clearly defined and motivated. At first, Perceval acts out of simple, irresponsible ambition, with no thought for the pain and suffering of others, particularly of his mother. Once he has "become" a knight, his thoughts turn toward his mother, in a rather rudimentary sense of responsibility, and he sets out to return to her. The third movement is both intriguing and important: when the lady (who, it turns out, is his cousin) explains to him the meaning of his experience in the Grail Castle, he grieves briefly, but not for his tragic silence in that castle. It is rather the death of his mother, related also by his cousin, which causes his sorrow (ending the quest for the mother and beginning the third movement). In the ensuing events, he will conduct himself as might any other knight in Arthur's court, setting out to find adventure ("Que querre et encontrer voloit / Aventure et chevalerie": vss. 4166-67), aiding a lady in distress, daydreaming of his beloved—but with no notion of expiating any offense he might have committed toward his mother or the Fisher King. But at the same time, Arthur has packed up his court and set out to find this knight whose reputation has inspired admiration and wonder in all quarters. This third section, concluding with Perceval's triumphal return to court, thus recounts his chivalric ascension and the success in court and in the world which he wanted in section one. He has now achieved fame so great that, instead of his seeking Arthur, as at the beginning, Arthur and his whole court will now go looking for Perceval.

Finally, if we may preserve a little longer our assumptions about the conclusion of the work, the final section should recount the successful conclusion of the Grail quest. There Perceval will not only demonstrate his responsible devotion to a cause (thus developing further the rudimentary responsibility he felt, in section two, toward his mother), but in a sense he will also conclude *both* sections two and four, since we learn that the failure to ask the Grail question was directly related to his guilt in regard to his mother's death. Thus, we may see a structure not of three movements but of four; the third, which is not Perceval's quest, but the quest *for* Perceval, seems to me an essential part of the work; it is the confirmation both of the hero's success as a knight and, by implication, of the inadequacy of the kind of chivalry he had long espoused. The moral dimension to Perceval's character is yet to come. And, as my summary and the following schema show, Chrétien interlaces these two themes—physical chivalry and responsible service, the quest for chivalry and the use of chivalry in a quest—in much the same way as he interweaves the adventures of Gauvain with those of the hero, introducing them and then interrupting them for the hermit scene.

Part I: The Discovery of Ambition
            (The Quest for Chivalry: Self-Centered Pursuits)
     Part II: The Discovery of Responsibility
            (The Quest for his Mother: Unselfish Actions for Selfish
            Motives)
Part III: Ambition Achieved
            (The Quest for Chivalry Complete: Fame, Reputation, Worldly
            Success)
     Part IV: Responsibility and Devotion
            (The Grail Quest; Resoluteness; Chivalry at Service of an
            Ideal)

Chrétien overlays a number of structures in his exposition of Perceval's story. More specific than either the interlacing of thematic movements or the general symmetry which points toward the center is a structure in four parts which is to be found within a good number of the episodes. That structure is 1) a departure, followed by 2) an encounter with a lady, then 3) a battle, which leads to 4) a return to court, usually by the defeated knight. With small differences in some cases (e.g., his second "encounter" with Blancheflor is only symbolic—in his reverie), the majority of episodes are so constructed, and the repetition of this structure permits the depiction of a progression, however small, from Perceval's abusive treatment of the Tent Maiden to his defense (although for selfish reasons) of Blancheflor. At the same time, the return of the defeated knights to court serves to spread the hero's fame rapidly and efficiently.

All careful readers of the work will have discovered additional patterns and correspondences (such as the relationship of Arthur's worldly court to the "other-worldly" court of the Grail Castle, or the ironic similarity of Perceval's inquisitiveness to his lengthy interrogation by Gornemant, who nonetheless cautions him against loquacity). Whether organized into patterns or not, the episodes of this work are more intimately related to one another by similarity of form, function, and imagery than in any of Chrétien's other works. Indeed, the web of analogical relationships in the *Perceval* is so extensive that the critic's job is as much one of selection as of analysis.

The most obvious and basic use of analogy throughout is of course in the simple recurrence of nearly identical scenes, such as those of Perceval's instruction—instruction given in similar fashion and overlapping substance by his mother, by Gornemant, by the hermit.[31] There is of course a hierarchy established from one of these scenes to the next, and the reader's inevitable recollection of the previous episodes in the series makes the progression from one level to another more strikingly apparent. The periodic recurrence of these instruction episodes calls to mind another recurring series of events, in which Perceval, who finds other pursuits more pressing, sends word to court that he will return *later* to avenge the smiling maiden whom Keu had offended. The two most significant of these episodes occur just before and just after the Grail Castle scene and its explanation by the maiden in the woods; they are the symmetrical episodes recounting his liberation of Blancheflor and his liberation of the Tent Maiden.

Although obvious analogical relationships undeniably exist among the scenes I have mentioned so far, the resemblance here is nonetheless so apparent as to make the term "analogy" practically useless. In numerous other situations, however, one scene varies the motifs of a preceding one, or duplicates a single aspect of another, or simply uses language to recall another. For example, Perceval's mother instructs him not to remain long with anyone without asking his name. From here on, asking someone's name, or failing to do so, will be important in a number of ways. Interestingly, Perceval does not even know his own name, and despite his extreme inquisitiveness about everything else, it does not occur to him to ask his mother who he is. Ironically, though, when he is required to give his name later, he manages to guess it. A permutation of the name motif occurs when Perceval first meets Arthur. The king is distracted by the theft of the golden cup, and, as he will later lament, he fails to ask the youth's name. The analogy of Arthur's failing to Perceval's is apparent, and indeed, if we take the cup as a symbol of the king's reign (as Hoffmann suggests: p. 87), his failure corresponds to Perceval's in a more precise way: just as Arthur's actions are due to his preoccupation with the symbol of his royal function, so does Perceval's obsession with the symbols and rules of chivalry cause him repeatedly to ignore advice and to neglect his reasonable moral duty.[32]

This reference to Perceval's flaw brings us to perhaps the most significant analogical construction in the first half of the poem—the repetition and variation of the delay and impatience motifs. Despite his mother's pleas, Perceval, in his eagerness to find Arthur and become a knight, refuses to delay his departure. Once established, this motif then becomes the nucleus of most of the major scenes to follow, for his immaturity and faulty perception of the nature of chivalry cause Perceval, as I have suggested, to postpone actions he should perform and perform immediately those he should postpone in favor of others. For example, at court, Keu strikes the maiden who smiles at Perceval, and recalling his mother's advice that he come to the aid of women in need (vss. 533-8),[33] we might expect the hero to avenge the maiden's injury. But Perceval is impatient to obtain a suit of armor and has no time for anything else. He simply swears to return later, and he leaves. As we will learn, such a reaction is entirely typical. It is true that he will later agree to remain at Blancheflor's castle and defend her from her enemies (although he is seduced, whether sexually or otherwise, into doing so); even here, however, after winning praise and glory in the battle, he will ignore his lady's sorrow and anger and soon leave to return to his mother. The delay motif is perhaps more prominent, and certainly more fateful, in the Grail Castle scene. There, the strange procession arouses Perceval's curiosity, but, recalling Gornemant's advice, he remains silent. His notion of appropriate behavior causes him to delay his inquiry until the following morning— when of course it will be too late. Chrétien concludes: "Si criem que il n'i ait damage" (vs. 3248).

Thus, up to the point where Perceval fails to ask about the Grail procession, he has passed up an opportunity to save his grief-stricken mother; he has offended and endangered the tent maiden and then departed without repairing the damage he has done; he has ignored his obligation to avenge the injury done the smiling maiden; he has been impatient to leave Blancheflor, despite her sorrow and despite the fact that she gave him her love and shared his bed; and finally, his delayed inquiry in the Grail Castle prevents his curing the Fisher King. His failings are of course related to his naiveté and ignorance of the world, but they are specifically due to his irresponsible refusal to let anything deter him from becoming a knight, seeking adventure, and following the physical code of knighthood.

While the nature of Perceval's sin is peripheral to my subject,[34] the discussion of analogical composition can clarify some aspects of the problem. We are told that he remains silent in the Grail Castle in obedience to Gornemant's instructions, but later we learn that his failure there is due to his earlier causing his mother's death. Of course, in the theology of the Middle Ages, an event can have both an immediate and a distant cause, and it is not surprising to find two explanations for Perceval's action.[35] But in spite of this theological justification it is nonetheless difficult to understand *how* his leaving his mother could cause his failure in the Grail episode, unless we simply conclude that his forsaking his mother predisposes him to sin later. But if a cause and effect relationship is not easy to establish, the two acts *are* related on the level of analogy, both by form and by Perceval's motivation. Quite obviously, he has not yet understood that chivalric adventure is meaningless unless its purpose is to serve others; chivalry for its own sake is vain. He is eager to acquire the tools of knighthood and follow its rules and he ignores all else. Thus, he is in haste to leave his mother and his home, to find King Arthur and procure a suit of armor. Later, Gornemant advises him that a knight talks little, and he dutifully remains silent in the Grail Castle. His motivation is the same in both scenes, and his departure from his home is simply the first in a series of adventures in which his faulty conception of knighthood will lead him to neglect his duty; the final and most serious of these adventures constitutes the crisis in the Grail Castle. At the same time, Chrétien's analogical method functions here, as it frequently does, by contrast: Perceval's impatience, his refusal to delay, in the first episode, contrasts with his intentional delay in the latter one. In both cases, his actions have similar results: in his haste to leave his mother, he causes her death, and by his postponement of the Grail question he fails to cure the Fisher King. Thus, while the causal relation between the episodes is elusive, Perceval's naive and faulty conception of chivalry simply establishes a pattern which he reinforces with the smiling maiden and with Blancheflor and which leads directly to his silence in the Grail Castle.

As I have suggested, we could continue at length identifying analogy at work in this romance. For example, Perceval's entry, on horseback, into the tent foreshadows his similar entry into Arthur's presence, and Arthur's silence, in turn, foreshadows Perceval's own. A number of parallels, including sexual ones, relate the tent scene to the Blancheflor episode. And Perceval's defense of Blancheflor and the resultant restoration of her land, by ironic contrast, point up his failure in the Grail Castle. This episode itself contains a large number of parallels to other scenes of the work, and we might, with Hoffman (p. 84), consider the Grail Castle episode to be a condensed analogy of the entire work. I have elsewhere mentioned the sword given to Perceval in this scene. It is the strongest and most beautiful sword in existence, and the resemblance between this physical symbol of chivalry and Perceval himself, by now the most capable and respected knight of the land, could hardly be without meaning. Furthermore, despite the extraordinary qualities of this sword, it is destined to break in the moment of Perceval's greatest need; thereafter, it can be repaired only by its maker. Thus it is with chivalry, symbolized by the sword: in ordinary situations it is more than adequate, but to meet severe tests it must be remade by a higher conception of love and devotion. Perhaps it would be going too far—or perhaps not?—to suggest a further parallel between the sword and the hero himself, for the latter also possesses a tragic flaw; he too will fail when he is severely tried, and the flaw can be repaired only by his own return to his Maker.

We should also note, in the same episode, that the blood on the point of the lance prefigures the three drops of blood on the snow, while the bleeding lance reminds us of the one which wounded the Fisher King (and recalls the *gavelos* first carried by Perceval). The Grail, of purest gold, is related analogically to another vessel, Arthur's gold cup. Finally, the helplessness to which Arthur is reduced by the theft of that cup corresponds in a general way to the condition of the Fisher King, whose restoration is related to the Grail.

In many instances, such as with the sword discussed above, analogy is far from the obvious technique it is in some scenes. For example, the episode which presents Perceval's reverie over the three drops of blood on the snow may even contain an incidental parallel to his causing his mother's death and then leaving, for the blood was that of a bird struck to earth by a falcon which then departed without pausing. The origin of the blood is hardly an important element of the episode, and in any case we may find the similarity of this situation to Perceval's own too vague and slight to justify our considering them analogues at all. But this is precisely the point: analogy so informs the entire work that it is rarely possible to define its limits and distinguish between a deliberate recasting of a motif and an incidental reflection of it. Once the work's themes and motifs are established, they appear to generate around themselves numerous episodes which incorporate them or reflect them in a variety of ways. Analogy is definite and obvious in some places, but it also consists of numerous and brief echoes in others. In the latter case, it functions merely as an *evocative* means of amplification, rather than as a precise and organized system of correspondences on a one-to-one basis. Few of these echoes bear an essential relation to the work's meaning, but the more of them we perceive, the fuller and richer the work becomes. They provide much of the texture, or resonance, of any medieval romance.

*   *   *

Critics have in recent years offered us numerous structural studies, many of them thorough and excellent, of Chrétien's poems. Certainly, after their work and my own suggestions in this chapter, the formal excellence of those poems requires no defense here. Chrétien shows himself as conscious of structural problems as any author, medieval or modern, and as much in command of his compositional resources. The physical patterns established in his works are surprising in their intricacy, and the ease with which he weaves together his frequently multiple and diverse narrative threads provides a convincing demonstration of his technical mastery. However, his most impressive accomplishment is to my mind his success in interweaving not just narrative threads but meaning, form, and the physical facts of the narrative, all in one coherent and satisfying whole.

Throughout this chapter, I have insisted, perhaps to tiresome extremes, on the poet's use of analogical composition. My justification is that I am convinced not only of its importance but of its priority in the construction of the romance narrative. For it is the nature of that narrative to seek diversity in its detail while fixing and reiterating in the audience's minds the theme or problem whose elaboration is the author's task. Thus, sub-plots and subsidiary themes may abound, but in practically every case they exhibit certain resemblances to the central theme. They are, as I have suggested, *somehow* related to it, even though causality does not frequently provide the link. The explanation for the prevalence of analogical composition may be sought in ideology (cf. Aquinas's remarks on analogy) or in psychology, where, prior to the fixing of the poem in print, relationships of *kind* appear to be the most common way of organizing phenomena and establishing their coherence. In any case, analogy is a most effective organizing principle in art, and it is certain that it is a very practical tool as well. Although the medieval audience, accustomed to narrative patterning and symmetry, would no doubt perceive certain elements of the physical arrangement of events, more elaborate patterns (such as the one Kelly traces in the *Charrette*) might well escape notice. Yet, there is every reason to believe that analogical relationships, the thematic and functional similarities among parts of the text, would impress themselves easily on the consciousness of the audience.

Chrétien's romances typically begin with a scene, important for the narrative development but without direct relationship to the hero's problem or situation, which constitutes a prefiguration or a burlesque of that problem. This thematically gratuitous episode seems to set the subject and direction of the narrative, and it is reasonable to suppose that an audience which expects analogical recapitulations of scenes will see this technique as an analogical prefiguration (by contrast or by exaggeration). That initial episode must be at least as important for whetting curiosities as are the interruption and postponement of events.

Briefly, in *Erec*, that prefiguration is offered by the scene in which Erec lags behind the other knights in the hunt, for he prefers to remain with the queen. In *Cligés* (a less clear instance than *Erec*), it may be Alexandre's hiding his intentions until he procures a "blind promise" from his father, or it may be found in the exhortation to spend and give away wealth openly and generously (prefiguring Alexandre's closed ways in regard to other subjects). *Lancelot* provides the best example of the burlesque analogy, when at the beginning of the work we see the queen prostrate herself before Keu in a remarkable illustration of the total and abject subservience which she herself will demand and expect from Lancelot. In *Yvain*, Arthur remains too long with the queen and falls asleep in her chamber—a situation which suggests that of Erec and which, causing as it does the grumbling and resentment of the other knights, illustrates the arguments used by Gauvain to separate Yvain from his wife. Finally, in *Perceval*, it is the hero's naive inquisitiveness which contrasts strikingly to his failure to ask the single question which would have saved the Fisher King.

Analogical composition is one of the most prominent methods by which Chrétien organizes his material and confers both form and meaning on it, and despite the incompleteness of the final poem and the number of problems which remain, even *its* structural coherence is impressive. An important element of Chrétien's fiction is the tension established by contrasts and polarities in his works. This is no less true of form than of theme. Thus, to impart meaning to the quest, he must establish a perceptible form, but he must do so without sacrificing random, chance adventures and the open, extendible, discursive style necessary to a quest romance. That perceptible form is frequently the creature of analogical composition. Gustave Cohen, dealing with Chrétien's work, spoke of

". . . aventures accessoires greffées sur la principale. . . ."[36] but the essential fact is that, while adventures *could* be grafted on or—for that matter— amputated, the episodes which find their way into the work are, by their form, function, imagery, or language, entirely appropriate to the poet's design. Thus, analogy plays an essential role in the creation of what Chrétien referred to, in *Erec et Enide*, as a *bele conjointure*.

CHAPTER V

CONCLUSION

Fiction as an art form is the narration of a series of situations that are so related to each other that a significant unity of meaning is achieved; the situations are presented in language such that at each point in the progress of the narrative the kind of relationship between retrospect and anticipation is set up that continually and cumulatively reinforces the desired implications of the plot, so that plot becomes symbolic as well as literal in its meaning.

That statement, by David Daiches,[1] is intended as a description of narrative fiction in general, but it provides an accurate description of Chrétien's art in particular. Out of variety (the episodic nature of Chrétien's works, the "series of situations") the poet derives unity; and although unity is a concept which must be applied to medieval literature with extreme caution, a unity of meaning in Chrétien's romances is evident. He is seeking a *sens*; he is examining chivalry in a literary attempt to discover the proper balance of the prowess, excitement, and adventure attached to that concept with the ideas of devotion, love, and responsibility, which his works propose as essential prerequisites for the valid cultivation of a knight's craft. Depending on the work and the point of view, we may see the particular nature of his examination as involving the relationship of love (and usually, marriage) to prowess or that of the individual to society, but in either case Chrétien is constructing fictional syntheses of two apparently contradictory notions. How are the active and the passive lives to be reconciled? How can the relationship of the couple be satisfactorily maintained in the face of the knight's responsibilities to the court, to society, to the tenets of his chivalric code? And in particular, how can that code be properly transformed from selfish (as Chrétien suggests it has become) into selfless (as his works suggest it must be)?

Chrétien's solutions to these problems (his "theses," if that word may be used without its moralistic implications) were obvious novelties for a culture accustomed to authors who beguiled their listeners with tales of adultery and adventure, in which lovers and knights outdid each other in the passion of the former pursuit and the daring of the latter. Chrétien made his heroes espouse a cause. They may devote themselves to a wife (or in *Lancelot*, a mistress) or they may wed a religious ideal, but whatever the local variations from one work to another, they do, after false starts, crises, and trials, serve a cause.

Novelties they may have been, but Chrétien's ideas are not profound. Indeed, although we as critics and students of literature may be reluctant to admit it, the ideas in our art are rarely if ever profound. Most themes border on the commonplace, or if they are new, it is usually only in the context of the culture in which they are produced. To tell us that Chrétien thought (in most of his works) that a man and woman who loved each other ought to be married to each other, or that the simple search for thrills and adventures was a vain pursuit, is to tell us little. What does distinguish literary art, or any other, is precisely its artfulness; that is, profundity resides less in what is said than in the way it is said, less in the thesis than in its elaboration. Or, less narrowly put, profundity resides in the harmonious relationship of the thesis to the properly organized components of its elaboration. Chrétien's achievement lies, in my view, precisely in his successful establishment of such a relationship. He is not simply telling a tale of adventure, nor is he indulging in didacticism. Rather, he is so constructing a narrative that its elements combine to posit (or better, to *become*) a valid thesis. It is the way he conjoins the discrete elements provided by his material which confers originality on his works, and with that reference to *conjointure* we return to questions of technique.

If Chrétien did not always have the freedom to choose his subject matter (as in the *Charrette*, for example), he nonetheless took great freedom in his narrative treatment of it. This is a freedom which Chrétien relinquishes only for good reason. When he as narrator limits his omniscience and neglects to tell us something, it is invariably in order to communicate something else, of greater importance. Otherwise, he is everywhere in his stories, commenting, explaining, directing; in certain cases he enters his stories to offer us knowledge denied to the characters themselves and to create a dramatic irony which illuminates his characters more effectively than a gradual exposition could have done.

Those characters continue to present interest, even though they may be no more than tools for the author's elaboration of a problem. A certain number of them evolve to a remarkable degree; others, not at all. Yet even some of the latter characters, static as they are, are traced and presented in sharp relief. If we except Perceval (Chrétien's most memorable construction) the poet appears to be at his best in the creation of female characters. Enide, Fénice, Lunete, and to a lesser extent Blancheflor stand out sharply against the well-populated background of Chrétien's work, and with the exception, again, of Perceval, Fénice is to my mind the most interesting of the poet's characters. It is not what happens to her, but the clarity with which her passion and obsession are drawn that makes Cligés pale beside her. Once again, Chrétien is notable not for the characters he creates but for the technique with which they are realized and presented.

Much of the poetic interest and value of Chrétien's works derive from perfectly balanced correspondences and symmetries within them. These can be developed to an elaborate and highly sophisticated level, but they also function in very simple, direct ways as well. The most elemental of structures in Chrétien's poems is that of plot, of the three steps leading the character typically to achieve, to lose, finally to regain his success and happiness, which usually means his chivalric integrity. This final step, the successful conclusion of his quest, may to the casual reader seem to be composed of a haphazard group of adventures bearing little relation to each other. This, as we have seen, could hardly be farther from the truth, for with the correspondences and symmetries I spoke of Chrétien organizes the work with a high degree of precision and patterned exactness.

T. B. W. Reid writes that "romances of adventure are necessarily episodic in structure, and often formless."[2] It is true that the episodic composition is an essential characteristic of many romances, and of course, *being* episodic, these works are freed from the requirements of further organization. Chance encounters and unexpected adventures are a necessary part of the knight's experience. Yet it is in the nature, if not of the narrative, at least of the poetic or narrative impulse to bring to the work additional organizing principles. Those principles, as I have enumerated them above, include diptych or triptych structure, symmetrical composition, centrality, interlace (whether the ABABA pattern noted by Kelly in the *Charrette* or the patterned interlace of *Yvain*), and others. And, of course, since the medieval mind tended to operated analogically (at least as much as logically), further relationships which involve analogies among the episodes or among certain elements of them are almost inevitable organizing characteristics of the romance.

If Chrétien's poems achieve a definite organization, they do not thereby sacrifice their loose, episodic nature. In fact, primary among the numerous tensions in which Chrétien's poems are suspended is that to which I have previously referred, the tension between centrifugal and centripetal forces. The first is the open, discursive character of the work; it is a force which resists organization. Against it is an organizing impulse which arranges the story in patterns and symmetrical sequences. Thus, one force is pulling the narrative apart by juxtaposing more or less unrelated episodes; the other is pulling it together by subtle organizational methods.

Dewitt Parker has isolated and studied six principles of esthetic form: the principle of organic unity, the principle of the theme (a dominant theme, pattern, or meaning which contains and reflects the whole), thematic variation, balance, the principle of hierarchy, and evolution.[3] With the exception of the first of these principles, we can see that all of them are embraced by Chrétien's art. A single dominant theme (which does not exclude subsidiary themes and sub-stories), its variation when reflected by different episodes and sometimes its inversion when it is anticipated or recalled analogically, the balance of one character against another or one event against another (and not infrequently the balance of whole sections of narrative against each other), the hierarchy established among the characters and especially in the sequence of adventures facing the hero, and finally the evolution of the theme and of the hero, whose obsessive purpose after the crisis is to cease being what he was, to become what he has not been—this list constitutes a capsulized description of a romance by Chrétien de Troyes.

The matter of organic unity is more complicated. If "unity" is a dangerous term, "organic" is doubly so. As Vinaver comments: ". . . 'organic unity' in the sense in which we commonly use the term is a metaphor traceable as far back as the 16th century, but not beyond, and not entirely valid for the 20th. Our failure to realize this has caused us to overlook the very things that give life and meaning to medieval literary art and to much of our own."[4] We should attempt, with Vinaver, to clarify the differences between medieval literary art and that of later periods, and thus it is perhaps best to expunge the term "organic" from our critical vocabulary when dealing with the Middle Ages. And yet, if the term were used to indicate (as it does in Parker's definition) that every element in a work of art is necessary to its value, the difference between medieval and "modern" is less one of organicism than of the *kind* of literary value sought by the poet. The medieval poem is a different kind of work which uses different techniques to arrive at a different meaning and value. Perhaps it is only a quibble, but we could argue that, since diversity possesses positive value in the romance, an episode which presents only a tenuous relationship to the main theme is an essential element in making the romance what it is. Remove an episode: the theme and thesis remain the same, but the work is not quite what it was before. Rearrange the loose-knit episodes of the quest: the character of the poem changes. In certain romances after Chrétien, this principle is *only* a principle; in Chrétien it is a fact, for the patterns and variations and progressions established among segments of the work contribute more to the character of the romance than do any individual episodes or sequences, however important.

This study of Chrétien's art is far from complete—an admission which the reader will recognize as more than mildly understated. My premise throughout has been that Chrétien was a self-conscious artist applying accomplished and effective techniques to his material. But form and content, method and material constantly refer to each other in his works, and consequently I have found it impossible to separate the fictional world he creates from the techniques by which its creation is achieved. Thus, while I have omitted much which might perhaps be included, I have discussed what I find essential: the nature of that fictional universe, its themes, problems, and conventions; the characters who inhabit it; the role of Chrétien as narrator in presenting the story to us; and his role as artist in creating and organizing that story. The romance, as fashioned by Chrétien, is an elaborate mosaic, fascinating and intriguing and frequently surprising in its subtlety. A poem written in the Middle Ages is a potential antique; a poem of Chrétien de Troyes remains a vital and fascinating artistic creation.

APPENDIX:

THE COMPOSITION OF THE *GUILLAUME D'ANGLETERRE*

In every period there are certain literary works which attract critical attention for other than literary reasons. The primary example of this phenomenon in the Middle Ages is Villon's poetry, which has held great appeal for antiquarians and for literary and social historians. Their contribution to our knowledge of that poetry has been enormous, of course, but their research leads, perhaps unwittingly, to the attitude expressed by Lanly, who rather baldly comments that these *travaux éminents* (meaning the successful identification of Villon's characters and allusions) leave little for later critics to do with his poetry.[1] Of such scholars, none has ever to my knowledge denied the intrinsic value of that poetry; their interest simply lies elsewhere.

For entirely different reasons, the *Guillaume d'Angleterre* has suffered somewhat the same fate. Here we are not dealing with a true masterpiece of literary creation, as we were with Villon, but it is nonetheless a work of great interest and not inconsiderable merit—and a work which has fascinated a certain number of critics primarily because of the problem of authorship. To the extent the poem itself is actually examined, it is usually to determine whether it is recognizably the work of Chrétien de Troyes. Here the matter of authorship, interesting though it may be, concerns me only indirectly. I suspect that it is a problem without a possible solution, and I prefer to dispose of it immediately by noting that I consider the work to have been composed by a poet of some skill, and I at least see no persuasive reason to *dispute* its attribution to Chrétien. There are two matters which seem more significant to me: the poem's character and its construction. Just what kind of work, in fact, is *Guillaume d'Angleterre*, and how is it put together? While these questions are apparently separate, they do overlap considerably, as we shall see.

The beginning of the romance can hardly avoid reminding us of saints' lives. It is most frequently related to the legend of Saint Eustache, because of factual similarities; for the purpose of literary comparison, however, it may be convenient to relate it to the more familiar Alexis story. Thus, just before an event which could be expected to bring great happiness (Alexis's marriage; the birth of Guillaume's children), the hero is obliged to leave his comfortable and prosperous world; he divests himself of possessions and goes into exile to lead a life of privation and misery, for the greater glory of God. Moreover, *Guillaume d'Angleterre* is replete with strange and marvelous noises, wondrous lights, and the voice from above—the messenger of God, reminding us again of *Alexis*. There are also striking descriptive similarities, despite the greater stylistic amplitude of the *Guillaume*.

Once Guillaume hears the voice, there begins a series of episodes in which he first repays those from whom he has wrongly taken anything, and then he gives away all his worldly possessions, before finally going into exile with his wife, Gratienne. But his trials are only beginning. He is happy when twins are born, but the family is hungry, and he is prepared, in a gesture of sacrifice and love, to cut off a part of his thigh to feed his wife. Then, in a rapid sequence of events, his wife is abducted, a wolf carries off one of his children, merchants find the other and take it away, and finally, an eagle swoops down and snatches the purse left him by his wife's abductors. He is left hungry, penniless, and alone, a situation in which Alexis would no doubt have exulted. But suddenly the narrative takes an entirely different direction, and its religious elements are largely forgotten. Three central divisions of the work permit us to follow the fortunes of Gratienne, the two sons (Marin and Lovel), and Guillaume himself. And here the word "fortunes" should be taken literally, for these sections relate the characters' ascension to affluence and power. Once this ascension is complete, they return to England to resume the life which God's command had initially caused Guillaume and Gratienne to abandon.

The central portion of the work is remarkable for the author's successful (if sometimes graceless) continuation of three or four separate narratives. But certainly the most significant fact about this section is God's absence from it. Once Guillaume leaves his homeland, he thinks rarely of God, and the forgetfulness is apparently reciprocated. The characters are on their own here: although Guillaume gives up all his wealth after hearing the voice from above, God does not require him to remain poor. When the characters have the opportunity to gain wealth or power, God is no longer a consideration. Nor are they prevented, once their fortunes are made and they are reunited, from returning to their homeland.

It is no doubt this thematic and moral discrepancy between the beginning and the body of the work which in part caused Frappier and others to see the poem as *décousu*. But an examination, however cursory, of the form of this romance will demonstrate that, at least from this point of view, the work is far from haphazard. Its structural configuration, while not notably complex, nonetheless exhibits a symmetry and balance which support the contention that the author was indeed a conscious and able craftsman. If that is the case, perhaps we should not so casually dismiss as flaws the thematic and tonal inconsistencies of the early part of the poem.

I have already summarized the initial situation of the work and the events which follow the characters' departure: after the twins' birth, the queen is abducted, the twins are taken away, and the purse left for Guillaume is stolen by an eagle. Following the central portion of the poem (to which I shall presently return), the purse drops from the sky, Guillaume is reconciled with his sons and then with Gratienne, and after necessary preparations, they sail for their own land and resume their initial position of power and wealth. The form of the first and last portions of the poem can thus be indicated by the formula ABCDE / XXXXX / EDCBA, with "A" representing the static situation existing at the beginning and re-established at the end. In other words, having worked itself into a pattern, the text turns around and works out of it. The result is a symmetrically mirrored framework for the body of the poem.

The central section comprises a series of episodes which possess their own structural and situational symmetry. The episodes devoted to each of the characters in turn are composed of blocks of narration two- or, most often, three hundred lines long. The symmetry consists of sequences in which each character has an opportunity to achieve a certain amount of security and success, which he however deems inadequate. Gratienne can marry a wealthy knight; she wants his land, we are told, but she remembers her noble rank and hesitates to lower herself to accept his offer. Almost as an afterthought, the author remarks that she thinks of Guillaume and wants no man but him. In fact, she works out an acceptable compromise: telling the knight (Gleolaïs) that she still has a year to run on a vow of chastity, she manages to marry him and inherit his lands without gracing his bed. The morality of her act is never questioned, and her husband conveniently dies before the year is out. Her two sons are apparently destined to become furriers, and though they know nothing of their noble blood, they reject this profession and leave their foster homes. Of Guillaume himself we are told that he makes himself so useful to his employer that he soon gains power; later, he is offered a position as seneschal in his own land, but he declines, protesting that he is unworthy, and eventually he returns as king instead. Each one spurns an apparent opportunity to improve his lot, and his refusal eventually leads to success greater than that opportunity would have afforded.

The exact center of the work (the structural center, which is separated by only fifteen lines from the physical center, at vs. 1655) divides two 300-line sections devoted to the sons; the second of these parts relates their departure from their foster homes. Notably, this is the point at which the sharply diverging lines traced by the characters' paths reach their widest separation and turn to begin a converging movement. In segments of the same length, Guillaume visits his homeland, in a passage I have already referred to; then, after a storm at sea, he comes to Gratienne's country, and they soon recognize each other. He next hunts in the neighboring land, where, by remarkable coincidence, his sons now reside. The stage is set for reconciliations, although a catalyst is required. The hostility which the sons show for their unrecognized father ceases to be a threat when the purse, plucked from before Guillaume twenty-four years earlier, now conveniently falls back to earth at their feet. Once the twins are convinced of Guillaume's identity, the reconciliation with Gratienne will not take long, and the characters are soon ready to return to England to reclaim the throne.

When we turn our attention to the meaning of the work, we encounter immediate difficulties. There is much in this poem that must strike us as artificial, and we may be particularly disturbed by the author's rather contrived use of providential events at pivotal points in the narrative. There is moreover a striking discrepancy between the beginning of the work and the rest, as hagiography is transformed into romance. Furthermore, our usual expectations are rarely met in this work, for when the characters react to the most dreadful misfortunes with deceit and deviousness, their experiences always end in triumph or success. As these comments suggest, irony is a prominent feature of the work. For the most part, it is a localized irony, occurring in statements made by the characters themselves. For example, when Gratienne receives the knight's marriage proposal, and when Guillaume is later offered a position as seneschal in his own country, they both protest that they are unworthy of such honors and that to accept them would be to rise too far above their stations.

In a technical sense, moreover, irony informs the entire romance, for the fact remains that it is not really about what it first appears to be about, and it does not develop as we are led to expect. Yet, despite the obvious disparities involved in the development of character, event, or structure, the *tone* of the work is most definitely not ironic, and there is neither implicit nor explicit authorial criticism of the characters or their actions. In fact, the poem provides an interesting critical problem in that it contains all the elements of literary irony without being fundamentally ironic in its conception and meaning.

After the pious tone of the story's opening sequence, God suddenly disappears, and from this point on the character of the work is radically altered. It soon becomes apparent that the real subject of the romance is neither piety (as the beginning might suggest) nor God's punishment of Guilluame (as the latter thinks), but simply how to get ahead in the world.

Specifically, the work's diverging-converging motion and the characters' descent and ascension appear designed to illustrate two principles proposed within the poem itself. First we are told that the person who humbles himself will be exalted (vs. 1024) and that one gives in order to receive (vss. 147-165). Such figurative precepts tend to be given a literal meaning in the poem, and they are accurately illustrated by the experiences of all the characters. Guillaume, notably, gives up all he has, but his poverty proves to be only the first step in his accumulation of the wealth which will eventually bring him back to his original state. The second of the work's principles or theses, a common one in medieval literature, is that *nature passe nourriture*; this too is applicable to all the characters, but especially to the two sons. The fact that they are ignorant of their royal origin is irrelevant. Nobility will out, and the characters eventually and (one could almost say) inevitably succeed in spite of the most formidable of obstacles. They are able as well as noble—or given, the aristocratic bias of the work, perhaps it would be more to the point to suggest that they are able *because* they are noble, a fact which the poem effectively illustrates. Parenthetically, it should be noted that the preachments of the story's *vilain* characters are generally the converse of those posited by the narrator; for example, Gonsselin (Lovel's adoptive father) assures Lovel that one's character is judged by the amount of money he has (vss. 1581-84). This may indeed be correct, but he neglects the more pertinent point made by this work: that one's material success is in fact *determined* by his character.

Given the premises of the romance, it does not seem to me unjustified to see it as a kind of *roman expérimental*. Characters of a predetermined nature are removed from a comfortable but static situation, deprived of possessions, security, and each other, and left to their own devices— which prove to be considerable. Throughout this section, the narrator tends to comment rarely, except to excoriate the *vilains*. The impression is that he is conducting an elaborate literary experiment, with significant social implications. This explanation may provide the most acceptable justification for the hagiographic nature of the beginning. If the author's purpose is to remove the characters from one situation in order to observe and depict their reactions in another, God's command that they leave their homeland accomplishes this purpose with remarkable economy.

But if this hagiographic character of the beginning conveniently leads us into the central situation of the poem, it also accomplishes much more, for it also establishes the work's psychological climate. A saintly or nearly saintly person is not to be judged by the same criteria as the rest of us. Any suggestion, for example, that Alexis is insensitive and cruel to his wife and parents would of course miss the point entirely. Whatever he does is in obedience to, and in the cause of, a higher authority, and his actions can be judged only by that standard.

In *Guillaume d'Angleterre*, this moral climate created from the beginning so conditions our response (unquestioning acceptance) that we are prepared to continue accepting the characters' actions in the middle section. There, the prerogatives of sainthood are simply replaced by the prerogatives of nobility. Accordingly, when the characters scheme, deceive, and lie, their acts are likely to be taken as normal and justified means to an end which is itself justified by the fact of their noble birth; the narrator presents these acts without criticism, and we are disposed to accept them the same way.

The brief ending of the poem, finally, constitutes not only a symmetrical pendant to the beginning, but a synthesis of the first and second parts. Thus, in spite of its difficulties, the romance offers an interesting example of the thesis, antithesis, synthesis dialectic developed frequently by Chrétien de Troyes. The characters begin from a position of power and wealth, but it is a position which they occupy by virtue of inheritance. The second movement is the exact opposite: they are deprived of everything and are left only with their personal worth. The conclusion depicts the restoration of their power, this time as a result of their own value rather than their birth. Thus, the ending of the poem represents a fusion of the physical form and some of the narrative content of the first part with the psychological and moral premises which dominated the central sequences. The work's aristocratic concerns have now replaced its religious values; the characters are noble and prosperous people who have thoroughly and convincingly demonstrated their personal worth and resourcefulness. God's function in all this is apparently that of a catalyst for the action, and when he has performed that function, he is conveniently dispatched.

Admittedly, while we are accustomed to certain tonal shifts and complexities in medieval literature, it is hard not to be disturbed by the heavily religious cast of the beginning, followed by the sudden disappearance of the Deity. We doubtless feel the tension which accompanies the change from saint's life to romance, but it is a tension related as much to our literary expectations as to any lack of internal coherence in the work, and in any case, the two contrasting segments of the poem are effectively fused at the end.

Everything considered, if the work is by Chrétien, it is a less impressive creation than any of his others, and it undeniably contains flaws which I have no desire to conceal. But that is not to deny its own value. In its physical and thematic structure it is quite effective. And although Frappier objects that the characters are "mus par la Providence comme des marionnettes" (p. 83), his judgment does not really do justice to the work; for although Providence is responsible for the transition from one section to the next, the characters themselves, as intelligent, resourceful human beings, direct their own fate within the large central sequence of the work. And as a literary experiment, the poem is clearly successful. It is scarcely a masterpiece, but critics who approach it in an attempt to discover the poem rather than its author will find their efforts justified.

NOTES—CHAPTER I

¹See Barbara Nelson Sargent, "L'autre chez Chrétien de Troyes," *Cahiers de Civilisation Médiévale*, 10 (1967), 199-205. Although I shall refer frequently to a character's evolution, we may best see this evolution as *quantitative*, as the character becomes "more" or "less" what he has been, rather than completely different. For a brief and excellent discussion of this question, see Evelyn Birge Vitz, "Type et individu dans l"autobiographie' médiévale," *Poétique*, 24 (1975), esp. pp. 430-31.

²"The Plot Structure in Four Romances of Chrestien de Troyes," *Studies in Philology*, 50, No. 1 (Jan., 1953), 1-15; see esp. p. 4. Of the works he treats, I omit *Guillaume d'Angleterre* from my discussion, except for the appendix devoted to it.

³*Cligés*, vss. 67-71. All my references to Chrétien's works are to the following editions: *Erec et Enide, Le Chevalier de la Charrete*, and *Yvain*, all edited by Mario Roques (C.F.M.A., 1973, 1970, 1971); *Cligés*, ed. Alexandre Micha (C.F.M.A., 1968); *Le Roman de Perceval, ou le Conte du Graal*, ed. William Roach (T.L.F., 1959); *Guillaume d'Angleterre*, ed. Maurice Wilmotte (C.F.M.A., 1962).

⁴This point is made, in regard to Perceval, by Pierre Gallais, *Perceval et l'initiation* (Paris: Les Editions du Sirac, [1972]), p. 51.

⁵"Multiple Quests in French Verse Romance: *Mervelles de Rigomer* and *Claris et Laris*," *L'Esprit Créateur*, 9, No. 4 (Winter, 1969), 257.

⁶See *Inferno*, V, 73-142; also *Inferno*, XXVIII, 139-142, where Dante has Bertrand de Born explain the term to the pilgrim.

⁷*Summa Theologica*, II, II, 61, art. 4.

NOTES—CHAPTER II

¹*Medieval Romance: Themes and Approaches* (New York: Norton, 1973), p. 147. Note also Frederick B. Artz, *The Mind of the Middle Ages* (New York: Knopf, 1953, 3rd ed. 1962), p. 376:

"So all human experience is packed with meanings at various levels, and one function of the writer, the artist, the teacher, and the preacher was to try to interpret the unknown from the known. Behind every object and every event lay a spiritual implication of which the immediate experience was merely the imperfect reflection. . . . the universe is a vast cryptogram to be decoded."

²Of the appearance of this Grail, we will learn that, in addition to being a resplendent object, it was a dish or vessel capable of holding a pike, lamprey, or salmon but containing instead a single mass-wafer (vss. 6420-23). For Helinandus, a Grail was definable as a *scutella lata et aliquantulum profunda* (see Migne's *Patrologia Latina* CCXII, col. 814). On the origin, development, and function of "Grail," see Roger Sherman Loomis, "The Origin of the Grail Legends," in *Arthurian Literature in the Middle Ages: A Collaborative History*, ed. Roger Sherman Loomis (Oxford: Clarendon, 1959), pp. 274-94; also Jean Frappier's *Chrétien de Troyes et le mythe du graal* (Paris: S.E.D.E.S., 1972), pp. 5-12.

³On the misinterpretation of signs in *Perceval*, see Rupert T. Pickens, *The Welsh Knight* (Lexington, Ky.: French Forum, 1977), pp. 83-86.

⁴For a penetrating discussion of certain aspects of Chrétien's symbolism, see Peter Haidu, *Lion-Queue-Coupée: l'écart symbolique chez Chrétien de Troyes* (Geneva: Droz, 1972).

⁵However, the fascination exerted by the Grail should not cause us to ignore the lance, a prominent element in the Grail procession and in the quest Perceval is undertaking when his story ends. D. C. Fowler relates the lance and Grail, respectively, to the two attributes indicated in his title: *Prowess and Charity in the Perceval of Chrétien de Troyes* (Seattle, 1959). Fowler may well be too categorical in his judgments, but by their very nature the lance and the sword which occupied attention earlier in the same episode are suggestive of the vocation which Perceval has undertaken with an immaturity which leads him into error. We should however note that even when Perceval finally learns the Grail secret, the hermit does not offer at the same time any explanation of the identity or meaning of the lance (although writers after Chrétien were not long in providing an explanation of their own). In addition, we should recall that the lance itself is apparently less important than the fact that it bleeds, and the question he is determined one day to ask concerns the reason for this peculiar characteristic of the lance. The blood is suggestively related to that which causes Perceval's reverie later, and in general the bleeding lance suggests wounds and unwholeness (whether of the Fisher King, his father, or—by symbolic extension— prowess). But if blood is the indication of wounds or death, it is also the stuff of life, and the symbolism of the lance assumes an extraordinary richness and an essential ambiguity.

⁶Jacques Ribard would of course disagree. In *Chrétien de Troyes: Le Chevalier de la Charrette* (Paris: Nizet, 1972), he notes not only the messianic dimensions of Lancelot's character, but also the imagistic similarities between the cart and the cross of the crucifixion. He then assumes that an object or character will represent what it suggests: Lancelot is Christ, the cart is the cross, Guenevere is the human soul. In my opinion, Ribard, like many allegorists of medieval literature, overlooks two important facts: 1) a medieval symbol is plurivalent (a characteristic which he does admit [p. 171] but which is scarcely implicit in his analysis); b) a distinction must be drawn between symbolic *meaning*, on the one hand, and resonances or symbolic *associations* on the other. Thus, the recognition of Lancelot's messianic dimension does not necessarily entail a religious interpretation of the character or work; the comments I make below (p. 21) concerning the lion as a figure (not a symbol) of Christ are applicable here as well. Lancelot is a Christ-figure, but I see no evidence that he is meant to be Christ. The cart is the cross on which he suffers, but it is not The Cross. As with Yvain's lion, the development of a messianic character does not necessarily entail a religious interpretation, but it does imply the use of a set of supporting images which might be considered religious in nature.

⁷The suggestion is Steven's, p. 147.

⁸For Paris, see *Mélanges de littérature française du Moyen Age* (Paris, 1910), p. 268. For a summary of the scholarship on this subject, see Julian Harris, p. 1143 of the article cited below, n. 9.

⁹"The Role of the Lion in Chrétien de Troyes' *Yvain*," *PMLA*, 64 (1949), 1143-63.

¹⁰See Harris, p. 1148.

¹¹See "Symbolism in Medieval Literature," *Modern Philology*, 56 (1958), 73-81.

¹²Gauvain does of course reappear for the final combat with Yvain, and interestingly, that is the one contest from which the lion is absent.

¹³Perhaps we might wish to see not two stages of development but three: Yvain is identified with Gauvain, then with the lion, then—at the end—he is sufficient unto himself, a fact indicated by the lion's absence. This suggestion, consistent with both character and theme, was offered me by William Kibler.

¹⁴A similar principle is at work when Dante sees Beatrice at the summit of Purgatory: poetic imagery and language suggest that we are witnessing an advent of Christ. But, as Charles Singleton remarks, there is in this "advent" no suggestion that she *is* Christ or that

she *represents* Christ. The poet establishes an analogy which stops well short of identity. See Singleton's *Journey to Beatrice*, vol. 2 of *Dante Studies* (Cambridge, Mass.: Harvard Univ. Press, 1958) pp. 73-75.

[15]*AEsthetic Distance in Chrétien de Troyes: Irony and Comedy in "Cligés" and "Perceval"* (Geneva: Droz, 1968), see pp. 64 ff.

[16]Alexandre's behavior is not uncommon for the love-sick hero of romance, but interestingly, the reactions of his son are different. He too is in love, and he too dwells at some length on his emotion—but without concretizing it in an external object. There are obstacles in the way of his love, but they are practical and political considerations and not, as they had been with Alexandre, a simple fear of love.

[17]See Gerard J. Brault, "Chrétien de Troyes' Lancelot: the Eye and the Heart," *BBIAS*, 24 (1972), 142-53.

[18]Glyn Burgess has suggested to me that this work *resembles* the others in presenting a conflict between individual self-indulgence (Lancelot and the queen) and the knight's social role. But he adds that circumstances make the resolution of this tension impossible, and to my mind it is precisely this incompatibility which sets the *Charrette* apart. In the other works love and adventure, the individual and the social can be reconciled; not so in the *Charrette*. Mickel notes that "Virtually every episode . . . illustrates that the real nature of honor often leads one to do things society brands as dishonorable. In the acceptance of apparent shame to one's self for the sake of others lies real honor." See Emanuel J. Mickel, "The Theme of Honor in Chrétien's *Lancelot*," *Zeitschrift für Romanische Philologie*, 91, Nos. 3-4 (1975), 245.

[19]*The Rise of Romance* (Oxford: Clarendon, 1971), pp. 31-32.

[20]I have kept the term "psychology," despite general disagreement concerning its applicability to medieval literature. Medieval poets were generally less concerned with psychological individuality than with types. According to Evelyn Birge Vitz (in "Type et individu . . ."; see above, p. 125, n. 1), the individual was seen in the Middle Ages as "le cas particulier d'un principe ou d'une idée universels" (p. 443), and she points out (p. 430) that medieval literature tended to emphasize a character's superiority or inferiority to a norm, but not his *difference* or exceptional quality. Nonetheless, it seems to me that the crisis and its aftermath (especially in the case of Yvain) are both psychological and ideological in nature (even if the hero is not different in kind from other individuals), and I do not consider cautious reference to psychology unwarranted. Psychological realism was not a concern of medieval writers, but this does not imply the absence of any psychological dimensions.

[21]For a brief discussion of Arthur, Keu, and Gauvain, see W. T. H. Jackson, "The Nature of Romance," *Yale French Studies*, No. 51 (1974), 19-20.

NOTES—CHAPTER III

[1]Chrétien de Troyes, *Arthurian Romances* (London: Dent, 1958), p. xvi.

[2]On the subject of Chrétien's critical terminology (*sens, matière, conjointure*), see W. A. Nitze, " 'Sans et matière' dans les oeuvres de Chrétien de Troyes," *Romania*, 44 (1915-17), 14-36; D. W. Robertson, "Some Medieval Literary Terminology, with Special Reference to Chrétien de Troyes," *Studies in Philology*, 48 (1951), 669-92; Douglas Kelly, "The Source and Meaning of Conjointure in Chrétien's *Erec* 14," *Viator*, 1 (1970), 179-200. In fact, *conjointure* is the only one of these three terms to present any serious problems of interpretation. Kelly's contention, that it is related to *iunctura* and that (p. 200) it ". . . is

specifically the result of the interlacing of different elements derived from the source or sources (or, for that matter, from the author's imagination)" strikes me as both useful and satisfying. His conclusion: "Arrangement and linking of narrative elements are therefore the essential objects of composition; even amplification and abbreviation and ornamentation are subordinate to that process" (p. 200). Whatever the precise process (the subject of my next chapter), *conjointure* clearly refers to the act and the processes of composition, to the operations performed on the poet's material so as to yield a particular meaning.

[3]In some cases the monologues are *exterior* in the sense that it is apparently Chrétien who is analyzing and discussing the characters' thoughts for us.

[4]Leo Spitzer, "Note on the Poetic and the Empirical 'I' in Medieval Authors," *Traditio*, 4 (1946), 414-22. My suggestions concerning Chrétien's individuality are contrary to the recent tendency to emphasize the collective aspect of medieval literary creation at the expense of the individual. Nonetheless, I think an exception must be made for Chrétien, whose use of "je" and "moi" appear designed to separate him from poetic collectivity.

[5]Vinaver (*Rise of Romance*, p. 38) indicates that the outcome of a battle is always in question. This is true in principle, but in fact, the battles which end in unpredictable fashion are rare. With few exceptions, the only surprising results of battles are their frequent postponement (Lancelot vs. Meleagant, for example); otherwise, our predictions of victory for the hero are generally accurate.

[6]Jean Frappier, *Yvain ou le Chevalier au lion* (Paris: Centre de Documentation Universitaire, 1952), p. 30.

[7]See *Erec et Enide*, vss. 1-26, esp. vss. 23-26:

> Des or comancerai l'estoire
> Qui toz jorz mes iert an mimoire
> Tant con durra crestïantez;
> De ce s'est crestïens vantez.

[8]In his study of *Æsthetic Distance in Chrétien de Troyes*.

[9]See William Nitze, "Erec's Treatment of Enide," *Romanic Review*, 10 (1919), 31-32; Z. P. Zaddy, "Pourquoi Erec se décide-t-il à partir en voyage avec Enide?" *Cahiers de Civilisation Médiévale*, 7 (1964), 179-85; William Woods, "The Plot Structure in Four Romances of Chrestien de Troyes," *Studies in Philology*, 50 (1953), p. 9. Jean Frappier attempts to reconcile the major theories in *Chrétien de Troyes* (Paris: Hatier, 1957), pp. 97-100.

[10]See my "Spatial Form in Medieval Romance," *Yale French Studies*, No. 51 (1974), 160-69.

[11]See above, n. 2.

[12]As Wayne Booth points out, reader sympathy tends to accrue naturally to any character to whom we have prolonged intimate exposure. See *The Rhetoric of Fiction* (Chicago: Univ. of Chicago Press, 1961), pp. 322-23.

[13]*Molt sainte chose* is vs. 6012. See below, p. 87 for her version of Saint Paul.

[14]Vss. 3113-14. For an early discussion of Fénice's attitude, see Gaston Paris, *Mélanges de littérature française du Moyen Age* (Paris, 1910; reprint 1966), pp. 287 ff.

[15]"Lancelot contre Tristan: La Conjuration d'un mythe subversif (réflexions sur l'idéologie romanesque au moyen âge)," in *Mélanges de langue et de littérature médiévales offerts à Pierre Le Gentil* (Paris, 1973), p. 618; Holmes's suggestion is made in *Chrétien de Troyes* (New York: Twayne, 1970), p. 78.

[16](Monte Carlo: Regain, 1963), p. 135.

[17]F. Douglas Kelly, *Sens and Conjointure in the "Chevalier de la Charrette"* (The Hague: Mouton, 1966), p. 213.

[18]Littérature et médiatisation, réflexions sur la genèse du genre romanesque," *Etudes Littéraires*, 4, No. 1 (April 1971), 70.

[19]*Chrétien de Troyes*, p. 87.

[20]But note that his undermining his prologue does not necessarily imply any criticism of Marie.

[21]In Fryean terminology, Perceval, in the course of his development, passes from the ironic mode ("inferior in power or intelligence to ourselves, so that we have the sense of looking down on a scene of bondage, frustration, or absurdity . . .") to the mode of romance ("superior in *degree* to other men and to his environment"). Whether the finished work would have taken him further, to the mode of myth (superior in *kind* . . .), is pure speculation, although that is the development that a number of critics suppose for the work. See Northrop Frye, *Anatomy of Criticism* (New York: Atheneum, 1967), pp. 33-34.

[22]For a brief restatement of their arguments, see Holmes's discussion in *Chrétien de Troyes*, esp. p. 158.

[23]Pierre Gallais (*Perceval et l'initiation*) appears to disagree, finding that attaching a special moral or religious significance to the Grail opens it up and enriches it; see especially ch. V, "Du Signifiant au signifié."

NOTES—CHAPTER IV

[1]*Etude sur le Lancelot en prose* (Paris, 1918), ch. 2.

[2]Eugène Vinaver, *Form and Meaning in Medieval Romance* (Leeds: Maney, 1966), p. 10.

[3]In addition to Vinaver's *Rise of Romance*, pp. 100-01, see Étienne Gilson, *L'Esprit de la philosophie médiévale* (Paris: Vrin, 1969), pp. 85-109.

[4]J. Huizinga, *The Waning of the Middle Ages* (London: Arnold, 1963), p. 185.

[5]Cf. Wolfgang Brand, *Chrétien de Troyes* (Munich: Wilhelm Fink Verlag, 1972), p. 10: "Das Grundprinzip des Strebens nach Einheit ist die Wiederholung."

[6]See my "Spatial Form in Medieval Romance," p. 169.

[7]Concerning this problem in two of the romances, see Robert G. Cook, "The Structure of Romance in Chrétien's *Erec* and *Yvain*," *Modern Philology*, 71, No. 2 (Nov. 1973), esp. 128-129, n. 5.

[8]I must admit that, like the majority of critics, I disagree here with Chrétien himself, for whatever his reason for terminating the first portion of the work at vs. 1796, the marriage represents both the thematic and structural completion of the "winning of Enide."

[9]I examine the quest episodes separately, see below, p. 75. But note that Z. P. Zaddy points out similarly that in *Yvain* the adventures which befall him are parts of a single episode in his development. See her *Chrétien Studies* (Glasgow: Univ. of Glasgow Press, 1973), p. 91.

[10]Süheyla Bayrav has offered an interesting structural analysis of *Erec*, as indicated in the following summary:

1. Brigands (2 combats): cupidité et brutalité
2. Galoin: luxure
3. Guivret: orgueil
        (Rencontre avec la Cour d'Arthur)
1. Géants: cupidité et brutalité
2. Oringle: luxure
3. Guivret: orgueil
        (Erec se prépare à aller à la cour)

1. "Joie de la Cour"

See Bayrav's *Symbolisme médiéval* (Istanbul, 1956), p. 97.

[11]In most medieval treatises on poetic art, such as those of Geoffroi de Vinsauf or Mathieu de Vendôme.

[12]See above, p. 45 for suggestions concerning motivation in the work. Clearly, Enide is acting out of concern both for Erec's reputation and for her own, and the quest thus functions both as an exoneration of the former motives and an expiation of the latter.

[13]It should be noted in passing that the Guivret episode depicts an intermediate stage in the proof of her love. When she once again warns him of danger in this episode, he threatens her, but we are told that, knowing she loves him, Erec has no desire to harm her.

[14]For certain details and suggestions in this regard, I am indebted to one of my students, Steven Gordon. He sees the work as possessing a basically tripartite structure overriding the bipartite, a length to which I would hesitate to follow him, but the point is well taken that the reactions of Cligés and particularly of Fénice do change markedly after his return.

[15]*Aspects of the Novel* (New York, 1927), p. 168.

[16]An example of the importance of a single word is *desafublez* (vs. 2713), discussed by Haidu, pp. 65-66.

[17]*Sens and Conjointure in the "Chevalier de la Charrette,"* pp. 166-203. However, Zaddy has serious reservations about Kelly's analysis; see *Chrétien Studies*, pp. 111, 150-56.

[18]In fact, the very structural pattern which Kelly identifies in the *Charrette* suggests the delay motif; his formula (ABABA; see especially pp. 173-84) refers to the interruption of an episode, which is then concluded only after one or more interpolated events.

[19]*Yvain ou le Chevalier au lion*, p. 8.

[20]As I suggest below, I see the quest as comprising six events: the defense of the Dame de Noroison against Count Alier, the encounter with the lion, the rescue of Lunete (an interrupted episode), the defense of Gauvain's relatives, the championing of the daughter of the Seigneur de la Noire Espine (interrupted), and the deliverance of the three hundred damsels. Zaddy, incidentally, sees the work as containing two main themes (The Winning of Laudine and The Estrangement and Reconciliation of the Lovers: *Chrétien Studies*, p. 101), three structural divisions, and seven episodic components. Moreover, she suggests that ". . . the various adventures which befall Yvain as the Knight of the Lion do, in fact, form a single episode in his life" (p. 91).

[21]See, for example, Gaston Paris, in *Mélanges de littérature française du moyen âge* (Paris, 1910), p. 268, n. 2: ". . . cette historiette [the lion]. . . ne sert à rien dans le récit. . . ." Paris elsewhere (p. 247) refers to Chrétien as ". . . un conteur adroit dans le détail, parfois maladroit dans l'ensemble. . . ."

[22]J. H. Reason, in his *An Inquiry into the Structural Style and Originality of Chrestien's Yvain* (Washington, D.C.: Catholic University of America Press, 1958), examines two structural principles of *Yvain* (tripartition and the gradation of adventures) but neglects the *entrelacement* which I discuss here.

[23]Frappier, *Yvain ou le Chevalier au lion*, p. 30.

[24]Chrétien neglects to explain how Gauvain came to champion a cause which he himself admits is wrong. Such an action may surprise readers who expect all Arthur's knights to participate in the same uncompromising morality that the hero comes to accept. Given Gauvain's character and his function in the work, however, it is clear that the episode is a further example of his accepting a task simply because of the promise it held of adventure and excitement.

[25]See for example Reid's statement: "The structural significance of the fourth component [the two sisters and the *tisseuses*] is uncertain, except in so far as it is evidently intended to

form a pendant and counterpoise to the introductory section [the story up to Yvain's marriage]." In Reid's edition of *Yvain*, p. xiii.

²⁶*Chrétien de Troyes et le mythe du Graal*, p. 256.

²⁷One of the scholars taking the opposite view—that the Perceval and Gauvain plots were originally parts of separate romances—is D. D. R. Owen; see ch. VII of *The Evolution of the Grail Legend* (Edinburgh, 1968). In *Two Old French Gauvain Romances*, ed. R. C. Johnston and D. D. R. Owen (New York: Harper and Row, 1973), the latter goes so far as to suggest that Chrétien was involved in the simultaneous composition of four romances: *Perceval, Gauvain, Le Chevalier à l'épée*, and *La Mule sans frein*; see p. 8.

²⁸See esp. pp. 103-05.

²⁹Stanton de V. Hoffman, "The Structure of the *Conte del Graal*," *Romanic Review*, 52, No. 2 (1961), 89.

³⁰Pickens (p. 49) refers to the Hermitage episode as "an incremental inversion of the poem's opening scenes."

³¹Related to these scenes are those in which, instead of instruction for his future conduct, Perceval receives criticism for past failings; those rebukes are dispensed by his cousin (after he leaves the Grail Castle) and by the hideous damsel who arrives in Arthur's court. (Interestingly, the latter arrives in Arthur's presence on muleback, reminding us of Perceval's own arrival at court.)

³²Notably, although Perceval did ask Gornemant's name, Gornemant, like Arthur, failed to ask *his*. Learning a person's name is apparently less a consideration for Perceval's new mentor than for his mother, who had instructed him: "N'aiez longuement compaignon/ Que vos ne demandez son non;/ Et ce sachiez a la parsome,/ Par le sornon connoist on l'ome" (vss. 559-62). It appears that in his progression from the natural to the social to the moral order, Perceval finds one level of conduct in conflict with another. The first level involved his natural inquisitiveness and his mother's advice concerning names, but his instruction on the next (chivalric or social) level intentionally excludes the inquisitiveness and omits the problem of naming. Perceval's cultivation of chivalry leads him to reject his former habits and precepts; in a sense the crisis results from the collision of the natural and social orders. His natural impulse, to ask the Grail question, is frustrated by his instruction in chivalric behavior. For a fuller discussion of conflicting levels of conduct in this work, see Hoffman, pp. 89-92.

³³We should not overlook the fact that, while Perceval exercises too much zeal in performing the other actions suggested by his mother, he fails in this one; not only does he fail to aid the smiling maiden immediately, but he fails to turn back to help his own mother when he sees her fall to the ground. Thus, his chivalric ambition imposes a tragic selectivity on his responses, and his first act on his way to becoming a knight is a sin which results from his disobeying her instruction.

³⁴For a detailed discussion of the hero's sin, see David G. Hoggan, "Le Péché de Perceval," *Romania*, 93 (1972), 50-76, 244-75.

³⁵Perhaps the best known example of this phenomenon is the conclusion of the *Mort Artu*, which presents the final tragedy as the immediate result of Mordret's treason, while the ultimate cause is the love of Lancelot and Guenevere.

³⁶*Un Grand Romancier d'amour et d'aventure au XIIe siècle: Chrétien de Troyes et son œuvre*, 2nd ed., rev. and enl. (Paris: Rodstein, 1948), p. 354.

NOTES—CHAPTER V

[1]*A Study of Literature* (Ithaca, N.Y.: Cornell Univ. Press, 1948), p. 55.

[2]In his edition of Chrétien's *Yvain* (Manchester: Manchester Univ. Press, 1961), p. xi.

[3]"The Problem of Esthetic Form," in *The Analysis of Art* (New Haven: Yale Univ. Press, 1924).

[4]*Form and Meaning in Medieval Romance*, p. 13.

NOTES—APPENDIX

[1]André Lanly, trans., Œuvres, by François Villon (Paris: Champion, 1969), I, xi.

[2]Frappier, in *Chrétien de Troyes*, p. 78; Gaston Paris, in *Mélanges*. . . , refers to the *Guillaume* as "la pitoyable rapsodie" (p. 45, n. 5).

SELECTED BIBLIOGRAPHY

The following bibliography is extremely selective. It is primarily a listing of the books and articles cited in the body of my study; I have omitted only the few items (e.g., Dante, Aquinas) which require no documentation and those of my own articles that are listed in the preface. Along with the remaining items, I have included here a small number of studies that I found particularly important or useful but that I had no specific occasion to cite.

For more extensive bibliographical reference, see Douglas Kelly, *Chrétien de Troyes: an Analytic Bibliography* (London: Grant and Cutler, 1976).

I. PRIMARY TEXTS

Chrétien de Troyes. *Erec et Enide*. Edited by Mario Roques. Classiques Français du Moyen Age. Paris: Champion, 1973.
_____. *Cligés*. Edited by Alexandre Micha. C.F.M.A. Paris: Champion, 1968.
_____. *Le Chevalier de la Charrete*. Edited by Mario Roques. C.F.M.A. Paris: Champion, 1970.
_____. *Le Chevalier au lion (Yvain)*. Edited by Mario Roques. C.F.M.A. Paris: Champion, 1971.
_____. *Le Roman de Perceval, ou le Conte du Graal*. Edited by William Roach. Textes Littéraires Français. Geneva: Droz, 1959.
_____. *Guillaume d'Angleterre*. Edited by Maurice Wilmotte. C.F.M.A. Paris: Champion, 1962.

II. SECONDARY MATERIALS

Adler, Alfred. "A Note on the Composition of Chrétien's 'Charrette.' " *MLR*, 45 (1950), 33-39.
Auerbach, Erich. *Mimesis: the Representation of Reality in Western Literature*. Translated by Willard Trask. Garden City, N.Y.: Doubleday, 1953.
Bayrav, Süheyla. *Symbolisme médiéval*. Istanbul, 1956.
Bednar, John. *La Spiritualité et le symbolisme dans les oeuvres de Chrétien de Troyes*. Paris: Nizet, 1974.
Bezzola, Reto R. *Le Sens de l'aventure et de l'amour (Chrétien de Troyes)*. Paris: Champion, 1968.
Bloomfield, Morton. "Symbolism in Medieval Literature." *Modern Philology*, 56 (1958), 73-81.
Booth, Wayne. *The Rhetoric of Fiction*. Chicago: University of Chicago Press, 1961.
Brand, Wolfgang. *Chrétien de Troyes: Zur Dichtungstechnik seiner Romane*. Freiburger Schriften zur Romanischen Philologie, 19. Munich: Wilhelm Fink Verlag, 1972.
Brault, Gerard J. "Chrétien de Troyes' Lancelot: the Eye and the Heart." *BBIAS*, 24 (1972), 142-53.
Brogyanyi, Gabriel John. "Motivation in *Erec et Enide*: An Interpretation of the Romance." *Kentucky Romance Quarterly*, 19, No. 4 (1972), 407-31.
Champigny, Robert. *Le Genre romanesque*. Monte Carlo: Regain, 1963.
Cohen, Gustave. *Un Grand Romancier d'amour et d'aventure au XIIᵉ siècle: Chrétien de Troyes et son oeuvre*. 2nd ed., rev. and enl. Paris: Rodstein, 1948.

Comfort, W. W., ed. and trans. *Arthurian Romances of Chrétien de Troyes.* London: Dent, 1914.

Cook, Robert G. "The Structure of Romance in Chrétien's *Erec* and *Yvain*." *Modern Philology*, 71, No. 2 (November 1973), 128-43.

Daiches, David. *A Study of Literature.* Ithaca: Cornell University Press, 1948.

Diverres, A. H. "Some Thoughts on the *Sens* of *Le Chevalier de la Charrette*." In *Arthurian Romance: Seven Essays*, edited by D. D. R. Owen. New York: Barnes and Noble, 1971, pp. 24-36.

Forster, E. M. *Aspects of the Novel.* New York, 1927.

Fowler, D. C. *Prowess and Charity in the Perceval of Chrétien de Troyes.* Seattle, 1959.

Frappier, Jean. *Chrétien de Troyes.* Paris: Hatier, 1957.

_____. *Chrétien de Troyes et le mythe du Graal.* Paris: S.E.D.E.S., 1972.

_____. *Yvain ou le Chevalier au lion.* Paris: Centre de Documentation Universitaire, 1952.

Frye, Northrop. *Anatomy of Criticism.* New York: Atheneum, 1967.

Gallais, Pierre. "Littérature et médiatisation, réflexions sur la genèse du genre romanesque." *Etudes Littéraires*, 4, No. 1 (April 1971), 39-73.

_____. *Perceval et l'initiation.* Paris: Les Editions du Sirac, [1972].

Gallien, Simone. *La Conception sentimentale de Chrétien de Troyes.* Paris: Nizet, 1975.

Gilson, Etienne. *L'Esprit de la philosophie médiévale.* Paris: Vrin, 1969.

Haidu, Peter. *Æsthetic Distance in Chrétien de Troyes: Irony and Comedy in "Cligès" and "Perceval."* Geneva: Droz, 1968.

_____. *Lion-Queue-Coupée: l'écart symbolique chez Chrétien de Troyes.* Geneva: Droz, 1972.

Hanning, R. "The Social Significance of Twelfth-Century Chivalric Romance." *Medievalia et Humanistica*, 3 (1972), 3-29.

Harris, Julian. "The Role of the Lion in Chrétien de Troyes' *Yvain*." *PMLA*, 64 (1949), 1143-63.

Hofer, Stefan. *Chrétien de Troyes: Leben und Werke des altfranzösischen Epiker.* Graz-Köln: Hermann Böhlaus Nachf., 1954.

Hoffman, Stanton de V. "The Structure of the *Conte del Graal*." *Romanic Review*, 52, No. 2 (1961), 81-98.

Hoggan, David G. "Le Péché de Perceval." *Romania*, 93 (1972), 50-76, 244-75.

Hunt, Tony. "The Structure of Medieval Narrative." *Journal of European Studies*, 1973, 295-328.

Holmes, U. T. *Chrétien de Troyes.* New York: Twayne, 1970.

Jackson, W. T. H. "The Nature of Romance." *Yale French Studies*, 51 (1974), 12-25.

Johnston, R. C. and D. D. R. Owen, ed. *Two Old French Gauvain Romances.* New York: Harper and Row, 1973.

Kellermann, Wilhelm. *Aufbaustil und Weltbild Chrestiens von Troyes im Percevalroman.* 2nd edition. Tübingen: Max Niemeyer, 1967.

Kelly, Douglas. "La Forme et le sens de la quête dans l'*Erec et Enide* de Chrétien de Troyes." *Romania*, 92 (1971), 326-58.

_____. "Multiple Quests in French Verse Romance: *Mervelles de Rigomer* and *Claris et Laris*." *L'Esprit Créateur*, 9, No. 4 (Winter, 1969), 257-66.

_____. *Sens and Conjointure in the "Chevalier de la Charrette."* The Hague: Mouton, 1966.

_____. "The Source and Meaning of Conjointure in Chrétien's *Erec* 14." *Viator*, 1 (1970), 179-200.

Köhler, Erich. *Ideal und Wirklichkeit in der höfischen Epik.* Tübingen, 1956.

Lacy, Norris. "Spatial Form in Medieval Romance." *Yale French Studies,* 51 (1974), 160-69.

Lanly, André, trans. *Œuvres,* by François Villon. 2 vols. Paris: Champion, 1969.

Lazar, Moshé. *Amour courtois et fin'amors dans la littérature du XIIᵉ siècle.* Paris: Klincksieck, 1964.

Loomis, Roger Sherman. *Arthurian Tradition and Chrétien de Troyes.* New York, 1949.

————. "The Origin of the Grail Legends." In *Arthurian Literature in the Middle Ages: A Collaborative History,* ed. Roger Sherman Loomis. Oxford: Clarendon, 1959, pp. 274-94.

Lot, Ferdinand. *Etude sur le Lancelot en prose.* Paris: Champion, 1918.

Lot-Borodine, Myrrha. *La Femme et l'amour au XIIᵉ siècle d'après les poèmes de Chrétien de Troyes.* Paris: Picard, 1909.

Luttrell, Claude. *The Creation of the First Arthurian Romance: A Quest.* London: Edward Arnold, 1974.

Maddox, Donald. *Structure and Sacring: the Systematic Kingdom in Chrétien's "Erec and Enide,"* Lexington, Ky.: French Forum, 1978.

Mickel, Emanuel J. "The Theme of Honor in Chrétien's *Lancelot.*" *Zeitschrift für Romanische Philologie,* 91, No. 3-4 (1975), 243-72.

Niemeyer, Karina H. "The Writer's Craft: 'La Joie de la Cort.' " *L'Esprit Créateur,* 9, No. 4 (Winter 1969), 286-92.

Nitze, William Albert. "Conjointure in *Erec,* vs. 14." *Modern Language Notes,* 69 (1954), 180-81.

————. "Erec's Treatment of Enide.' *Romanic Review,* 10 (1919), 26-37.

————. " 'Sens et matière' dans les oeuvres de Chrétien de Troyes." *Romania,* 44 (1915-17), 14-36.

Olschki, Leonardo. *The Grail Castle and its Mysteries.* Berkeley: University of California Press, 1966.

Paris, Gaston. *Mélanges de littérature française du Moyen Age.* Paris, 1910. Reprint Paris: Champion, 1966.

Parker, Dewitt. *The Analysis of Art.* New Haven: Yale Univ. Press, 1924.

Pauphilet, Albert. *Legs du moyen âge: études de littérature médiévale.* Melun, 1950.

Payen, J. C. "Lancelot contre Tristan: la conjuration d'un mythe subversif (réflexions sur l'idéologie romanesque au moyen âge)." In *Mélanges de langue et de littérature médiévales offerts à Pierre Le Gentil.* Paris, 1973, pp. 617-32.

Pickens, Rupert T. *The Welsh Knight: Paradoxicality in Chrétien's "Conte del Graal."* Lexington, Ky.: French Forum, 1977.

Press, A. R. "Le Comportement d'Erec envers Enide dans le roman de Chrétien de Troyes." *Romania,* 90 (1969), 529-38.

Reason, J. H. *An Inquiry into the Structural Style and Originality of Chrestien's Yvain.* Washington, D. C.: Catholic Univ. of America Press, 1958.

Reid, T. B. W., ed. *Yvain,* by Chrétien de Troyes. Manchester: Manchester Univ. Press, 1961.

Ribard, Jacques. *Chrétien de Troyes: Le Chevalier de la Charrette.* Paris: Nizet, 1972.

————. *Le Conte du Graal (Perceval).* Paris: Hatier, 1976.

Robertson, D. W. "Some Medieval Literary Terminology, with Special Reference to Chrétien de Troyes." *Studies in Philology,* 48 (1951), 669-92.

Roques, Mario. "Pour l'interprétation du 'Chevalier de la charrette' de Chrétien de Troyes." *Cahiers de Civilisation Médiévale,* 1 (1958), 141-52.

Sargent, Barbara Nelson. "L'autre chez Chrétien de Troyes." *Cahiers de Civilisation Médiévale,* 10 (1967), 199-205.

Singleton, Charles S. *Dante Studies.* Vol. 2 (*Journey to Beatrice*). Cambridge, Mass.: Harvard Univ. Press, 1958.

Spitzer, Leo. "Note on the Poetic and the Empirical 'I' in Medieval Authors," *Traditio*, 4 (1946), 414-22.

Stevens, John. *Medieval Romance: Themes and Approaches.* New York: Norton, 1973.

Uitti, D. Karl. *Story, Myth, and Celebration in Old French Narrative Poetry, 1050-1200.* Princeton: Princeton Univ. Press, 1973.

Vinaver, Eugène. *Form and Meaning in Medieval Romance.*, Leeds: Maney, 1966.

———. *The Rise of Romance.* Oxford: Clarendon, 1971.

Vitz, Evelyn Birge. "Type et individu dans l''autobiographie' médiévale." *Poétique*, 24 (1973), 426-45.

Woods, William. "The Plot Structure in Four Romances of Chrestien de Troyes." *Studies in Philology*, 50, No. 1 (Jan. 1953), 1-15.

Zaddy, Z. P. *Chrétien Studies: Problems of Form and Meaning in Erec, Yvain, Cligés, and the Charrette.* Glasgow: Univ. of Glasgow Press, 1973.

———. "Pourquoi Erec se décide-t-il à partir en voyage avec Enide?" *Cahiers de Civilisation Médiévale*, 7 (1964), 179-85.

Zumthor, Paul. *Essai de poétique médiévale.* Paris: Editions du Seuil, 1972.